Ulysses

A play for young people

John Wiles

Samuel French – London
New York – Toronto – Hollywood

PRINCIPAL NAMED PARTS

Poseidon	Hermes
Hecabe	Tiresias
Polyxena	Siren
Ulysses I	Secretary
Ulysses II	Calypso
Ulysses III	Telemachus
Zeus	Penelope
Athene	Antinuous
Cyclops	Eumaeus
Aeolus	Eurycleia
Circe	Chamberlain

Also **Soldiers** (who become **Sailors** and whose number include the **Bosun, Quartermaster** and **Helmsman**) **Refugees, Circones, Lotus-Eaters, Sheep, Pigs, Magic Cattle, Ghosts, Seagulls** *etc. etc.*

*

Acknowledgement is made that extracts have been used from Shakespeare's *Richard II* and *Troilus and Cressida.*

COPYRIGHT INFORMATION

(See also page ii)

SYNOPSIS OF SCENES

ACT I

SCENE 1   The Fall of Troy
SCENE 2   The Voyage Begins
SCENE 3   The Lotus-Eaters
SCENE 4   The One-Eyed Cyclops
SCENE 5   The Kingdom of the Winds
SCENE 6   Circe and the Isle of Pigs
SCENE 7   The Land of the Dead
SCENE 8   Back to the Land of the Living
SCENE 9   The Sacred Cattle of the Sun

ACT II

SCENE 1   The Conference
SCENE 2   Calypso's Island
SCENE 3   Ithaca
SCENE 4   The Reunion

THE MAGICAL VOYAGE OF ULYSSES

Troy has fallen ...

The captains and the kings depart, some like Nestor to a happy home-coming, others like Agamemnon to a bloody one. As for Ulysses, he is condemned to ten years of exile for offending the gods during the siege. The story of his wanderings is well-known. Homer told it all in marvellous detail in *The Odyssey*.

The Magical Voyage of Ulysses was first presented by Group 64 in their theatre in South London, and later by the Heatham House Youth Theatre in Twickenham in Middlesex. Both productions had casts of between 30 and 40; in the first, the ages ranged from about 15 to 22, and in the second, between 13 and 16. Both casts were, of course, mixed. Both took place in the body of the theatre, rather than just on the stage, with the audience grouped on three sides, for great emphasis was laid on large-scale mass movement. Indeed rehearsals always started with 45 minutes of warm-up exercises, together with mime and dance work to prepare the casts for what was to come. Some of those sessions are described in the production notes.

This present version is probably more verbal than either of the earlier scripts if only because movement is almost impossible to describe. It can only be *done*. But ample opportunity is provided in the action for movement of all kinds, from joyous romps by young casts to highly intricate dance by those more ambitious. There is no present music track available. I made my own, using lots of Stravinsky, Mahler, Villa-Lobos and most interestingly Bernard Herrmann who composed music for many of the Hitchcock thrillers; now there was a composer who knew how to keep his audience on the edge of their seats!

Few companies can provide a cast this size without doubling. That is to be welcomed. I hope every actor plays dozens of parts! To me a performer sitting in a dressing-room is a wasted performer. I'd much rather he was forever changing his or her costume and coming back again and again, sometimes just to watch the others, if not actually perform. With the same intention I have split the part of Ulysses into 3 so that at least other members of the company can have a go. If the director wants to go further and divide it into 5 or even more, fine. Needless to say, some of these should not necessarily be played by males only.

Finally a note on the material. *The Odyssey* has been described as a poem, a novel, a history. It has also been called an allegory and a myth. It is each and all of these, which is probably why it provides such a wonderful stimulant to the youthful imagination. Of course the very word Odyssey now means "a long journey" and is frequently used to describe one's progress through life. Did Homer mean that? Did I? I don't think so, although it was difficult to resist the temptation at times, particulary when talking about the Cyclops or the Lotus-Eaters. I think the interpretation is up to each director; better still up to each director after long discussion with the actors. Whatever, what is provided here can only be a launching pad for your own ideas. Have fun with it.

In conclusion I know I ought to have called him Odysseus, but Ulysses always seems to come more trippingly off the tongue.

J.W.
London, 1990.

ACT I

SCENE 1

The Fall of Troy

In the darkness the mirror-ball begins to glow and spin, faster and faster, filling the whole hall with stars. A deep groaning is heard, bass and profound and rather metallic, as if the earth itself is splitting apart under our very feet. Mist swirls. A voice speaks greatly amplified

Poseidon (*on amplifier, clear and deliberate*) I am Poseidon, God of all the Seas, Lord of the Waters that cover the earth and flow beneath it. Not a ripple breaks on the furthest ocean but I have knowledge of it. The winds howl at my command. The waves and surf rear like horses at my slightest wish. Now hear this, O Zeus and all you other petty gods of heaven, hear this my curse.

A Light begins to grow in the mist revealing, as high as possible, Poseidon on his dolphin throne, holding his trident in his hand. This figure does not speak, but remains still and threatening as the amplified voice continues from off stage

Troy was my city, that jewel, that paragon of beauty. In its infancy I nursed it and nurtured it and watched it grow to splendid manhood. Then the barbarous Greeks came and with infinite greed tried to steal it from me. For ten long years we resisted their attacks, until by cunning and deceit they filled their Wooden Horse with troops, and infiltrated our trusting walls. Once in, they spread like some loathsome foul disease through all the heart and limbs of my beloved offspring. Now it seems it must die. Curse them, I curse them, Zeus, those light-fingered Greeks who came like thieves in the night to steal my city from me. And of them all, I curse the most, that lying Odysseus that some call Ulysses, who leads them with such cunning and duplicity, two-faced, a liar and a trickster.

Somewhere in the dark a drum begins to beat, steadily, ominously

Hear me now, O brother Zeus. My patience is at an end. If Troy falls— as fall it must—I'll lay such disasters on the conquering Greeks—and above all on that treacherous Ulysses—they would think themselves cursed for being born at all. My sea will rage, my winds blow always from the wrong direction, my rocks will pierce and splinter their frail craft into an hundred pieces, and above all, you Ulysses, will be doomed to wander at my behest *for all time* rather than reach your home. Hear me and

beware, Greeks. Take heed, Ulysses. If my city falls, you have made me
an enemy forever! A wanderer you'll be for all eternity.

*Thunder. The drum quickens. In the distance a new sound arises—that of a
city at war: men's voices shouting, the cries of the wounded, the clashing of
weapons and the crashing of buildings. As the Lights fade on Poseidon,
searchlights sweep the floor in all directions. The stars fade out and in the
distance perhaps a cut-out of the walls and towers of Troy with the red glow
of smoke and flame behind. The drum speeds up*

> *Watching his chance as the searchlights sweep across the floor, a Greek
> officer races into the hall and crouches in the shadows. The searchlights
> sweep close by—he freezes—then away again. He waves. Another Greek
> soldier joins him. Clasping swords or spears they wait in the shadows. As if
> suspecting their presence the searchlights grow more and more desperate.
> More soldiers arrive and begin to move up through the hall towards the city*

*The noise of the battle grows louder. So does the drum. Now music is added,
big chords with kettle drums and trumpets*

Officer Keep back, keep back. And low. Mind the lights.
Soldier 1 I'll take the Temple. There'll be gold there, mark my words, all
kind of loot.
Soldier 2 It's Helen I want. They say she's the most gorgeous woman alive!
Soldier 1 Too good for you then.
Soldier 2 Don't you believe it.
Officer Fools, be silent. Just concentrate on the work in hand. (*He stands*)
Now, Greeks, for the glory of the homeland, CHARGE!

*They all rise and advance up the hall in a combined movement, involving
stabbing and lunging gestures, accompanying each step with monstrous battle-
cries of rage. The Lights move frantically over them, sometimes fading to near
darkness, then coming up again through sickly greens to midnight blues. The
mist continues to flow. The sound of the battle increases. The slashing of
swords, the stabbing of spears, the plunging movements of the shields, now all
resemble a kind of virile dance of robots, as if working together they have
become a single killing machine rather than a number of individuals. Now a
new sight emerges: As the soldiers move steadily on the city . . .*

> *Refugees come from it, men as well as women, some carrying children or
> wounded comrades, all with bundles done up in rags, moving through the
> slaughtering Soldiers in an attempt to escape from the town*

*And just as the Soldiers have their battle-cries, so these too have their desperate
moans and shrieks as they flee for safety. To all, if the eardrums can stand it,
add thunder, more drums and for good measure . . .*

Poseidon (*amplified as before*) Beware, Ulysses. If the city falls, I curse you,
curse you, curse you . . .!

*A huge wind is heard, and as if sweeping all other sounds before it, the music,
drums, the noise of battle fade away*

The Soldiers go, leaving the hall to the Refugees

The Refugees sink to their knees in grief and suffering. Some call out weakly for help, others search for their families. One Woman calls out over the general keening

Woman 1 Where is my little son? Oh, my child, oh, my beloved, oh, my sweet lamb ...
Woman 2 They took my husband and cut him into a thousand pieces before my very eyes ...
Child Mother? Mother? Has anyone seen my mother ...?

The others take up the theme which grows into a general lamentation and just as the Soldiers worked as a combination so now too we see a general group of grief and disaster, lit perhaps by flashes of lightning. In the distance Troy flames and then slowly darkens

Man 1 Look, look, the city dies.
Woman 3 The Greeks have killed it. Oh, Troy, my beloved ...
Man 2 Will we ever see its like again? Will we ever return?
Woman 4 Return? How should we return? Where can we go now and what will there be to return to? I have lost everything.
Others (*almost like birds calling*) And I ... and I ...
Woman 5 So have we all.
Woman 1 Where is my little son? Tell me, kind sir, have you not seen a little lamb of a boy, five years old, skin like honey and hair like sun-ripened wheat ...?
Man 3 Alas, no, good mother.
Man 1 Hark, what is that?
Others Yes, listen ...

They turn and look

Hecabe Gone, all gone. And my home, my lovely city ...
All (*separately*) It's the Queen ... Hecabe! Quick, let's go to her!

They run to her and try to comfort her

Hecabe No, let me lie here in the dust. All is lost. The sons I bore were heroes to a man and their father too, Priam, more a god than man, has followed them to their graves. With these eyes I saw him hacked to death by Greek swords. Now they seek my daughter Polyxena. Weep, Troy, and cursed be the men that brought you to this end.
Polyxena (*a young girl*) No, Mother, they shall not have me. I'd rather die than fall into the enemy's hands.
Hecabe So would we all, my child, but the gods have left us no room to choose. Listen!

A chanting is heard off. They all take fright

All (*separately*) Quick, the Greeks are returning. Look to the Queen and her daughter .. hide them ... hide them!
Soldiers (*off*) Uly-sses! Uly-sses! Uly-sses!

The Soldiers sweep back carrying Ulysses on their shoulders. They look battle-soiled and weary. After all, they have fought ten long years for this moment and still can't believe it's happened. Some are not completely sober, others are still in a state of shock. Ulysses however is noisy and triumphant, his beard stained with wine

Ulysses How now, bully boys! What say, what say? Did I not promise you the day would be ours?

Soldiers Ay, ay, you did! you did!

Ulysses And was I not right? Has Troy not fallen?

Soldiers Ay, ay, you were right!

Their wild rush has brought them face to face with Hecabe. They are still carrying Ulysses. He has already spotted the Queen

Ulysses So, Split-Lip, so, Cross-Eyes, are you not the greatest soldiers in the world?

Soldiers Ay, master, that we are ...

They set Ulysses down. He moves to the Queen

Ulysses Well, Hecabe, is your daughter ready?

Hecabe Must you take her, Ulysses? I spared your life once. Can you not do the same for her? I found you once in Troy, spying for your army, a pitiful wretch in rags, covered with blood. I knew you, but did not call the guards. Instead I let you go to meet Athene to make a contract to spare the city. Spare us now, great Ulysses. You promised me once to remember the favour.

Ulysses I cannot. The commanders have agreed Polyxena must be given to Achilles, our greatest warrior.

Hecabe But Achilles is dead! Must she marry a corpse?

Ulysses (*a shrug*) In his grave. I cannot help it.

Hecabe Then I curse you, curse you, curse you, foul treacherous Greek. Everything you say is corrupted with lies.

Ulysses (*to some of his men*) Separate them and take them out. Then lead the girl to the ships.

They obey, some of the Soldiers leading Polyxena off

(*Pointing to the fading skyline*) See Poseidon's city is no more. See how it sinks into the sea.

Soldier (*worried*) Ay, Poseidon's sea.

Ulysses (*quickly*) What's that you say? Poseidon's? That god of the wet waters? Well, what of it? Do you fear him? Do you even take note of what he says? Well, tell me, do you?

Another Soldier (*uncomfortably*) He is a god, General, is he not? ... and brother of the great god Zeus himself.

Ulysses Ay, and I'm a general and with Agamemnon and Menelaus did I not seize Troy and trample it in the dust *in spite of him*?

Soldiers (*reluctantly*) Ay ... ay ...

Ulysses Over ten long years was it not I who buoyed up your hearts when life grew rough? And in the end was it not I who persuaded your other leaders to adopt the device of the Wooden Horse that won us the war?

Soldiers (*more confidently*) Ay, ay, you did ...

Ulysses And when the Horse was dragged inside the city, was I not among the commandos in the belly, and the first to drop out and lead the assault on the temple?

Soldiers (*persuaded*) Ay, ay, you were!

Ulysses Then what power have these gods say I! Let Poseidon fret and fry. We are men confident in our own strength and knowledge of our destiny! Pay them lip-service by all means, but hold on to your independence as human beings. They call it trickery and lies. I call it courage. After all, we have to survive.

Cheers from the Soldiers but a whisper passes amongst the Refugees

Refugees Blasphemy ... blasphemy ... blasphemy ...

Ulysses What is that, that dry crackle that runs like a flame in the undergrowth?

Man 1 Blasphemer! The great Ulysses is no more than a heretic.

Woman 1 Blasphemer! Spare us, lord Poseidon, we're not part of this!

Ulysses What's that they say? (*Furiously*) Seek them out!

Soldier It's nothing, lord, only some paltry refugees squeaking their tiny protests against history.

Others Here are more of them. Belt up, you puny beggars. Spiders and ants! Bugs, the lot of you. Stamp them out!

Soldier Shall we kill them?

Ulysses YES!! NO!! YES!!

Uproar everywhere

Refugees Spare us, Zeus! ... Hear us, Poseidon! ... O gods, has it come to this? ... (*etc.*)

Ulysses (*a stentorian shout*) NO!! Spare them! If only for a moment, spare them. Let them speak.

The uproar is quelled. In the brief silence

Soldier (*to the audience*) Don't misjudge him. It's not that he can't make up his mind. It's just that he sees so many sides to every question, he reckons up every probability at once!

Man 2 (*a sneer*) Don't you believe it. He's a commander who can't make a decision and as everybody knows, that's no commander at all. (*To the audience*) See for yourself. His great god's expediency.

Ulysses Silence! You there, you've got a great mouth on you. Speak! Tell me what you know.

Man 2 I? If I've got a great mouth, it's only because I bow to the gods. And you've heard what Poseidon has sworn. We all know it. By taking his city—his city—you have offended him. Now you've added insult to injury by defying him.

Refugee True ... true ... we want no part of this.

Man 2 That's what my great mouth, says, Lord. Apart from that, I'm

nought but a wretched refugee, the lowest of the low in your soldiers'
eyes ... scum as they are.

Soldiers Kill him! Hear how he speaks of us!

Others Yes, kill him! Kill him!

Ulysses Stop! Enough of this!! What he says is partly true. The lord Poseidon
did warn me and I defied him. Blasphemer, you called me. Well, that's
true, up to a point.

Soldier (*to the audience*) Oh, he has a great way with words! When it comes
to speeches, you can't beat our general.

Ulysses It's true he's a god and I'm only mortal, but there comes a time
when even a little man must stand up, inflate his chest and bawl defiance
at the stars. I know that, you know that and the gods know it. And they
like it. They like a show of defiance. It shows we want to be like them.
So we'll go home again despite Poseidon's warning. And soon! Today!
Watch and see!

Woman 2 (*unbelieving*) You challenge the gods?

Ulysses I do.

General reaction

That's the great difference between you and me. That's why I'm a great
commander, a leader of my people, a king and bounty lord of my tribe
of Greeks. So I say what I have said. Come, away! Some of you go
prepare our ships for sailing. Others, clear this rabble from my path and
kill only those who hinder you. The rest go to the city and fetch the prize
that has been promised me. No less a treasure than the Trojan queen has
been given me as a bride. Go! After ten years squatting here, I can't wait
to shake the dust of this pitiful land from my feet.

Soldiers Come, you heard! Now move!

*A general movement. The Soldiers drive the Refugees out. Others go up to
the city*

Man 2 (*one last shout before he leaves*) You'll regret this, Ulysses, to the
day you die!

Ulysses That may be sooner than you think, friend.

*At last he is left alone. The Lights go down to hold him in a single spot. After
a while he turns to the audience*

A blasphemer? Yes. A general who can't make up his mind? They may
be right. A way with words, cunning, a liar, a schemer? Yes, they may all
be right. But can a man change what he is, and if all those things are
Ulysses, then that is what I am, for I am Ulysses. Ten long, weary years
we've lingered here. The Greeks and Trojans have always been sworn
enemies and when a Trojan prince kidnapped a Greek princess, of course
we had to take up arms to get her back. The only pity was, it took us so
long. So many men have died, great men, heroes the lot of them—Achilles,
Hector, Great Ajax, Little Ajax, Diomedes, even Priam, King of Troy—
and now we're all that remain. By deceit we conquered them in the end
and they'll never forgive us, but justice had to be done so now we reckon

we have a right to go home. Wouldn't you agree? After all, we didn't start the blessed war. I mean I didn't want to come. You wouldn't think to look at me, but I'm a peace-loving chap at heart. Peace-loving Ulysses they used to call me in the old days. After all, I've a wife like any other man waiting for me at home, and a son Telemachus, growing up in my absence. So can you blame me for defying the gods and wanting to get home? I mean, would you think better of me if I just sat down and accepted my fate? Go on, be honest. Would you? Of course you wouldn't. And in my place, wouldn't you do the same thing? Of course you would. You know you would. After all, we're only human.

A rather fussy civilian man hurries through dressed in a nondescript suit

Ulysses looks at him in disbelief

Hallo, who are you?
Zeus Zeus.
Ulysses Zeus who?
Zeus (*rather North Country*) Just Zeus, lad. You know, King of the gods, that Zeus.

Ulysses falls to his knees

Ulysses Great lord! (*After a moment*) Are you sure?
Zeus Sure? Of course I'm sure. You know we gods can take any shape we've a mind to, a swan, a bull, a shower of gold. You shouldn't go by appearances. You know that.
Ulysses (*humbly*) Great god, I'm Ulysses. Odysseus to some, but Ulysses to many.
Zeus Ay, I know that. To tell the truth you're a great trial to us, lad, a great trial. Oh, you're a cut above the average all right, but you can't leave well alone. That's your trouble.
Ulysses Should I not have conquered Troy then?
Zeus Oh, I'm not saying that. You know as well as I do, we gods can't allow ourselves to take sides in the affairs of men, but to insult my brother the way you've done, fair beggars description.
Ulysses (*offhand*) Oh, Poseidon understands me, lord. He and I are much the same. He knows I say these things, but I don't mean them, just as he doesn't always mean them. But the common man demands these things. He likes to be frightened. Deep down Poseidon knows I respect the gods.
Zeus I'm not so sure about that, lad. I think he's got it in for you now, right and proper. Oh, you've got a way with words, I give you that, arguing this way and that, but this time I reckon you've gone too far.

A Light reveals Athene, dressed in white on the high spot earlier occupied by Poseidon

Athene Be careful, Zeus.
Ulysses Athene, goddess of Troy!
Athene (*drily*) I'm surprised you recognize me. You've broken your word to me so many times. I thought you'd decided to defy me also.

Ulysses You? Never. Oh, great goddess, in my heart——
Athene We know all about your heart, Ulysses. You've told us about it so many times.
Zeus Now look here, daughter. I'll have none of this. This matter is between Poseidon and myself——
Ulysses And me?
Zeus Well, I suppose so——
Athene And me!
Zeus No, no, no. Now your uncle insists that——
Ulysses I know! Poseidon has forgiven me!
Athene Ha!
Zeus Forgiven? Never. Not on your life, no, no.
Ulysses Not even a little bit?
Zeus Well, perhaps just a little bit. Just a scrap, you might say.
Ulysses Oh, thank god ... Zeus!
Athene Don't be too hasty, Ulysses. Now, Father, what do you mean?
Ulysses I knew it. I knew the gods can see right into a man's heart. They know when he's talking just for the sake of talking ...
Zeus (*to Athene*) What it boils down to is, in return for certain favours from me, he's agreed to cut down the wandering from *all time* to ten years.

The Soldiers return with their weapons and kit ready to embark

Ulysses That's not so ... TEN YEARS??
Soldiers Ten years? Ten bleeding years?
Zeus Ay, ten years it is. You see we feel that ought to be quite enough to teach you a lesson. A little patience and a little politeness. That's what you seem to lack.
Ulysses Ten years! But we can do that trip in four or five days!
Zeus Then you'll have to find some other way of filling in your time. Now I'm off. I've a meeting to discuss the disposition of centaurs in Arcadia in the next century and it's almost that now. Good luck to you all. And *bon voyage*.

Zeus goes

Athene (*calling after him*) And don't forget, you've given your word to Poseidon, Father! (*To the audience*) He'll short-circuit it, if he can. Ulysses was always a favourite of his. Well, now, Ulysses, isn't it time to embark? You haven't got far to go, but you've got a great deal of time in which to do it.
Ulysses Great goddess, won't you help us? (*With huge innocence*) What have I done to offend you?
Athene How can you ask? You know perfectly well that before the city fell we met in secret and you promised to spare as many of the citizens as you could. You also agreed to spare the city needless destruction. But when the time came, you forgot everything and led the vandalism and bloody slaughter yourself. And you ask what you did! Oh, Ulysses!
Ulysses (*apologetic*) That's war, I'm afraid.

Athene And so is this! Now you pay for it. Ten years of exile and victim of whatever Poseidon chooses to throw against you. Ten years! Oh, and don't worry about your family. I won't give them any information but I'll see they come to no harm. Off you go now, great general and great blasphemer. Even ten years won't last forever!

The Light fades on her

Another Soldier approaches Ulysses

Soldier More bad news, general. That Trojan Queen you were promised as a prize—it seems she had other ideas. When they killed her daughter, she cut her throat rather than go with you.
Ulysses (*the classic cry*) O, woe! Woe is me! The gods have abandoned us! What shall we do?
Soldier If you ask me, it's all for the best. They say it's bad luck to take a woman on board.
Another Soldier And over ten years who know what could've happened?
Ulysses (*instantly recovered*) Well spoken, lads. Then what are we waiting for? To the ship! Maybe we can beat old Poseidon after all. Everything's always for the best.

They hasten to the rostrum or ramp that is to serve them as their ship and throw their gear aboard. While they are going through their mime of rigging the mast and sails, Ulysses calls Ulysses II to his side

Time for you to take over. I'm worn out.
Ulysses II Already? I thought it wouldn't be till much later. Anyway I don't know a thing about sailing.
Ulysses Nothing to it. You pull on this, pull on that and shout a lot of incomprehensible orders. The crew do the rest. Piece of cake.
Ulysses II No, thank you, not for me. In any case we still have need of that famous cunning. You got us into this. Now get us out.
Ulysses (*flattered*) Cunning, eh? Ah, well, if you say so. (*He goes to the ship*) Look lively, lads. Aboard with you. Haul up the anchor and cast off. I must say I don't like the look of that sky ...

The Soldiers, now the Sailors, cast off, mime putting out their long oars and take up their positions, one leg firmly forward, the other back

And ROW!!

SCENE 2

The Voyage Begins

They start to row strongly, throwing the weight well forward over the front foot, then hauling back on the invisible oar, shifting the weight on to the back foot, using long spines. The Lights change to golden and narrow down on the boat. The mist has gone and the drums give a long, steady beat, perhaps accompanied by music having a strong, lyrical theme

Sailors (*in time to the rowing*)
                    O-eeoh O!
                    O-eeoh O!
                    Row, lads, for Ithac's shore,
                    The cursed Trojans we'll see no more.
Sailor 1 I remember my father's farm, golden in the sunset, the clean taste of milk and honey, fresh bread, and then a night's sleep under a clear sky.
Sailor 2 I remember my wife's blue eyes, her laughter as she nursed the children, her warmth when the nights turned cold.
Sailor 3 My daughter's smile when I came home from work reeking of the day's labour, the way she hastened to untie my sandals, the calm way she wiped my face.
Sailor 4 I've lived alone ever since a babe. The woods were my home, the foxes and wolves my childhood companions. I learnt to love nature as my own, the smell of forests after rain, the sweet touch of snow as I snuggled down to sleep.
Sailor 5 The raw taste of real Ithaca wine.
Sailor 6 Our grapes were always the best in the world.
Sailor 7 Our roast lamb was always roastier.
Sailors Our seas and cliffs even coastier.
Ulysses Row, lads, row.
Sailors   O-eeoh O!
                    O-eeoh O!
Sailor 8 Keep this up and we'll soon be home!
Sailor 9 First we'll see the lighthouse on Pharos Point——
Sailor 10 And then the windmill by old Clyton's place.
Sailor 1 My wife will be there hanging up the washing. She'll wave to us——
Sailor 2 And carry the news back to the others.
Sailor 3 "The lads are coming home!" she'll say——
Sailor 4 "Not today or tomorrow but soon ... soon ..."
All (*separately*) Soon ... soon ...

One by one they remember their predicament and lose heart. One by one they stop rowing. The music has gone

Sailor 5 Ten years!
Ulysses Row, boys, row!
Sailor 6 Do we have to keep this up *for ten years*?
Sailor 7 No Pharos Point?
Sailor 8 No Clyton's place?
Sailor 1 And my wife will not be here to wave to us ...
Sailor 9 Or worse, she'll be there and you won't.
Sailor 10 And then the message to the village will be "The lads are not coming home. Not today, not tomorrow, not ever!"
Sailor 1 Or not for another ten years which is as good as never!
Ulysses For the gods' sake, row, lads! I don't like the look of these rocks. We're drifting too close inshore——

Cries of alarm as they see what is happening

All (*separately*) Watch it! ... oh, no ... row ... (*etc.*)

They lurch as the ship grounds noisily

Ulysses Quick, scramble ashore before we sink! What land is this anyway!

Pandemonium as they save themselves

Sailor 2 I think it's the country of the Circones, sir.
Ulysses II (*taking charge*) In that case hurry! Light watch fires and post sentries. These people are dangerous, almost savages!
Ulysses Just a moment, just a moment. Who's in charge here? (*Shouting*) Well, hurry! Light watch fires and post sentries! (*To Ulysses II*) I thought you didn't want to do this bit.
Ulysses II Somebody has to be practical.
Sailor 3 Look out! Here they come!!

The rest of the cast drop out of the darkness, swing in on ropes, leap off boxes—all with terrifying cries and shrieks. They wear weird masks and gibber like monkeys

The drums crash and roll. The Lights go to almost nothing. The Sailors reel back under the attack. All seems to be stabbing and slashing

Ulysses Quick—back to the ship!
Ulysses II Too late, they've cut us off.
Ulysses Our warriors will beat anyone. Remember we're the best in all Greece!
Ulysses II *Were* the best, *were*! The oldest and tiredest now!
Ulysses What's it matter? Fight, boys, fight!

All of a sudden the attackers have gone

The crew is scattered, shocked and beaten. Groans and cries and then a long silence. Finally ...

Sailor 4 What was that?
Sailor 2 I told you. They're called the Circones. Savages. Cannon-balls.
Sailor 5 Cannibals, you fool.
Sailor 6 More like devils from hell, if you ask me. Look, they've taken our food. And the last of our wine.
Sailor 7 Do we have to go through ten years of *this*?
Ulysses II (*assuming command*) Enough of this. Quartermaster, take a party out to find food.

Some Sailors go off

Bosun, prepare the ship for sea. The rest of you, stand guard. We must not be caught out so easily again. (*To Ulysses I*) Give me the beard. I am Ulysses now.

Ulysses I unhooks the curly beard and retires to become one of the crew

Did we defeat the Trojans just to become fodder for all the low-lifes of the world? Get organized, boys, and be of good heart. Are we not the beloved of Ithaca?
All Ay, that we are!
Sailor 8 The old man is himself again.
Sailor 9 And so are we all. God rot old Poseidon and his curses.

A menacing roll of thunder

In a manner of speaking.

Sailors 1 and 10 return

Sailor 10 I've got food.
Sailor 1 And I've got wine.
Ulysses II Then to the ship. We'll sail at dawn.

The Lights go down to night. Then fade up slowly to dawn. With them comes the sound of a rising wind. Sailor 2 wets his finger and tests the direction of the wind. Ulysses II, now simply called Ulysses, joins him

Ulysses Well?
Sailor 2 North-easterly. Bound for Cythera. It's not what we want.
Ulysses It's all we've got. To the ship! Run it off the beach and let's get going!

They follow his instructions, embark and row again. The music returns

Poseidon (*on amplifier*) Oh, no, you don't! Take this!

The wind increases

And that!

And increases still more

Ulysses Good! That's what I wanted. Set sail, lads. Helmsman, steer south by south-west. There's a current there called the Big Fish. It'll take us down past Cape Malea and half-way home. Jump to it, boys!
Ulysses I I thought you didn't know anything about sailing?
Ulysses Every man knows more than he thinks he knows! Keep close-hauled, helmsman. Here we go!

They stop rowing and hang on for dear life as the vessel skims the waves

Sailor 3 It's better than flying!
Sailor 4 It *is* flying. I can see the stars beneath us.

The Lights go to deep night. The wind and music fade out. The stars fill the hall and cross and recross the ship

Helmsman Admiral, we've passed the Cape.
Ulysses Then steer due north for Ithaca. We'll soon be home now.
Sailor 5 Then we've beaten Poseidon!
All (*a huge cheer*) E-jus! E-jus!
Ulysses Well, come on, helmsman, *turn*!

The Helmsman strains on his steering oar. They wait expectantly

Helmsman Sir, I cannot. The current's too strong ...!
Ulysses I (*to Ulysses II*) You and your Big Fish!
Ulysses Everybody try!

They all scramble to help the Helmsman

Now! And again! Again!
Sailor 6 It's no use. We can't turn it!
Sailor 7 And now we're being swept out to sea! Say a prayer for us, sir!
Ulysses A prayer? Would you like that?
Sailors Oh, yes, sir, please, sir!
Ulysses Very well. "Great lord Poseidon, I'm sorry for the trouble I caused
and promise to do better the next time. P.S. Please send favourable wind
to get us home." How's that? Very important to keep on their good side,
you know.
Sailor 8 (*to Sailor 9*) Was that it?
Sailor 9 Better to have said nothing if you ask me.

They settle down for sleep. In the distance soft North African music plays

SCENE 3

The Lotus-Eaters

Ulysses (*to the audience*) For nine days we rode over the fish-filled sea and
on the tenth reached the Land of the Lotus-Eaters.

All becomes dream-like. The Lights keep low. The music itself is soporific

The Lotus-Eaters enter quietly carrying bowls of fruit

Sailor 10 Are we awake or is this a dream?
Lotus-Eater 1 Sometimes dreams are more real than reality.

The Sailors stir and go to meet them

Lotus 2 There is always more pleasure in dreams.
Lotus 3 Eat, mighty Ulysses, eat the fruit of dreams.
Lotus 4 There is no need of hurry.
Lotus 5 You have all the time in the world to linger.
Lotus 6 You could stay here for ten years and dream the time away ...
Lotus 7 Why not? By sending you here Poseidon has done you a favour.
Sailor 1 (*drugged*) A great favour ...
Sailor 2 A great favour ...
Lotus 1 Just eat. And dream. Dream ...
Sailor 3 Dream ...
Sailor 4 There is no hunger, no thirst ...
Sailor 5 No hot, no cold ...
Sailor 6 No time, no place, no light, no dark ...
Sailor 7 Just nothing ...

Sailor 8 Nothing ...
Sailor 9 Is this Paradise?
Lotus 2 What else? It's all Absence. No life, no death.
Sailor 10 Paradise ...
Lotus 3 The gift of the gods. Take it. Enjoy it.
Ulysses (*struggling to keep awake*) No, no, enough! This is not for us. True, life is pain but it's also joy. If there's fear, there must also be love. Away! Away! We must away before we become nothing. Quartermaster! Quartermaster!
Ulysses I What, turned moralist then?
Ulysses This is not survival, but surrender. Quartermaster, round up the men. Those who will not come, clap them in chains. If they resist, kill them!
Ulysses I Kill them? Why not just leave them here?
Ulysses To rot? Would you rather your great army should become *nothing*? Quartermaster!
Quartermaster Ay, I heard, but I can hardly move.
Ulysses (*rushing at him with a sword*) Then die, too, you apology for a Greek!
Quartermaster (*hastily*) WAKE UP, YOU SHIFTLESS SCOUNDRELS! Grey ghosts of a forgotten past, to the ships, blast you, or else choose— the irons or the sword!
Ulysses Quick, Poseidon sleeps! We'll make landfall before he wakes. He'll never find us then.

On amplifier, Poseidon chuckles

Ulysses I You'll be lucky. He's found you already.
Ulysses But he hasn't caught us.

The Men have been rounded up. They embark reluctantly and take up their oars, hustled by the Quartermaster and the Bosun

Lotus 4 This is not goodbye, Ulysses.
Lotus 5 You can always return.
Lotus 6 We'll be here waiting for you.
Ulysses Never! To escape life is not to live in it.
Lotus 7 The colours are brighter ...
Lotus 1 The sounds sweeter ...
Ulysses There's nothing sweeter than living! (*To the crew*) Row, curse you, or give your livers to my sword.
Quartermaster Row!
Bosun Row!
Ulysses Row!
Crew Row ... (*They begin to row again*)
                              O-eeoh O!
                              O-eeoh O!
Sailor 1 For a little while I thought I'd found peace.
Sailor 2 You did. But it was the peace of the gods, not man.
Ulysses Row!

Crew   O-eeoh O!
                                      O-eeoh O!

The wind comes up again. So does the rowing music

Sailor 3 Hear that?
Sailor 4 The old god's blowing off again.

The Lotus-Eaters have regrouped. Now they circle the ship and "wash" in towards it as "waves"

Sailor 5 Look, the current's turned. We're going north again.
Sailor 6 To Ithaca?

Ulysses and the Bosun are consulting a map

Bosun I know the place. It's wild and rough. The folk who live here are quite uncivilized. See how the mountains run down to the sea. That's the mark of a bad place.
Ulysses Still we'll have to put in for food and water.
Bosun (*a shudder*) I shouldn't risk it, sir. Not here.
Sailor 7 There's a thick fog coming, admiral.
Sailor 8 Like a curtain cutting us off from the land.
Ulysses That'll save us then. Steady, lads, lie low. I've told you everything works out for the best. Let her drift ...
Sailor 9 What is this place, sir? It makes my blood run cold.
Ulysses I know it now, the land of the Cyclops, the one-eyed monster more beast than man.

SCENE 4

The One-Eyed Cyclops

Sailor 10 Must we go here, sir?
Ulysses We've no option, lad. The gods sent us here.
Sailor 1 But they weren't doing us a favour, were they?
Ulysses They never do. It's up to us to turn what they send to our advantage ...
Sailor 2 I can't see anything in this fog. There is a stillness over everything. Am I alone in this world?
Sailor 1 Even the admiral's gone. We are drifting in a sea of mist, floating ...
Bosun Just one stroke then. One only ...
Sailor 2 Where will it take us?

They row one stroke

Bosun (*very firm but quiet*) Rest oars. Let her drift, lads, and make no sound. She'll touch bottom shortly.

They wait. A slight sigh

There she is. Over you go and no noise, mind.

Sailor 3 (*afraid*) Bosun, I can't see where to go.
Bosun Take my hand, lad. All join hands then. I'll lead the way. After you,
    sir.
Ulysses God bless you, Bosun. I'll take your hand.
Bosun As you say, sir.

*They weave their way ashore in a long line. The "waves" are standing now
and form trees, bushes, natural features on the island. The Sailors move
cautiously as if in a dense fog, led by the Bosun with Ulysses coming next.
Even though we can see them clearly, we must get the impression they have
placed their fate in the hands of the Bosun who is feeling his way over the
rocks, across a chasm, through a river and up a cliff. All the time they sweat
and pant and exhort one another—"Watch out, there's a precipice there!",
"Careful of that loose rock" and so on. Somebody stumbles or a stone is
dislodged and they all freeze in fear. This journey can go on a long while until
all the possibilities have been exhausted. Finally . . .*

    I think I see a light.
Ulysses Where?
Bosun Beyond those trees.
Ulysses Keep the men here. I'll take a look. (*He moves ahead*)

*The "rocks" regroup themselves. While the Sailors sink down to rest, Ulysses
moves on to tackle the new surroundings. As he reaches his objective, some of
the "rocks" form a small coral which he enters cautiously. During all this,
there has been no drumbeat, no music, no wind. All has been done in complete
silence. In silence also Ulysses explores the coral. Finding it empty, he returns
to the entrance and waves to the others*

Sailor 4 Zeus be praised. I think the fog is lifting . . .
Sailor 5 I can see the master. Bosun, he's calling us on.
Bosun I can see him, lad. Well, come on now, but remember, no noise.

They run up the quick way to join Ulysses. He ushers them into the coral

Ulysses It's a shepherd's shelter, but it will keep us warm and dry for the
    night.
Sailor 6 Thank you, sir. We can do with that.
Ulysses Bed down now. I'll stay on guard till midnight and watch over you.

*They find places to settle and in a moment all is still. Then we hear it: a single
drumbeat*

    (*To the audience*) Say what you like, you miss a lot just staying at home.

Another drumbeat

    Hallo, there it is again. I thought I heard it earlier.

Drumbeat . . . count 5 . . . another

    Something's coming.

He goes into the coral and wakes the Bosun who wakes the Men. The "footsteps" are approaching more loudly now and rather quicker. The crew brace themselves

Sailor 7 What can it be?

Sailor 8 I'll tell you what it sounds like—my mother-in-law.

Accompanying the footsteps, a new sound. After a certain amount of confusion it sorts itself out into something recognizable

Sailor 9 Listen——

Baaing

—sheep.

Sailor 10 If that's the shepherd with them, lord knows what he looks like.

Bosun Steady, boys. Keep down and very, very still . . .

Sailor 1 (*a whisper*) Bosun . . .?

Bosun (*ditto*) What is it now?

Sailor 1 There's a lot of grub here—cheese, wine, the lot. Can't we just grab it and scarper?

Bosun Too late, boyo, here he is.

The Sheep appear first, baaing loudly, and scrambling up the hillside to the entrance of the coral where they wait, nudging one another and making a terrific racket. Polyphemus the Cyclops follows. He is played by the tallest person in the company or preferably by two people, one sitting on the other's shoulders. He wears a tattered gown and a mask with gauzed-over eyeholes and a single glaring eye in the middle of his forehead. He is, to put it mildly, every child's favourite nightmare

Cyclops (*to the Sheep*) There, there, my little ones. Go inside and make yourselves comfortable. Your father will be along in a minute.

The Sheep cavort and frisk and dash inside where several are brought up short by the sight of humans where no humans have ever been before

His poor old bones are not as agile as they used to be, but a slice of cheese and a tankard of wine will soon put that to rights, I dare say.

Some of the Sheep seem to be squealing in excitement

How now, what's to do, Clarissa? How so, Morbidia? What's all the fuss? Pleased to see your old dad, eh? (*He stoops to pull their ears . . . then stops. Looks. Listens. Sniffs. After a while*) Fee fie foh fum, I smell the blood of an Englishman . . . (*He sniffs again*) No, not English, too sweet for that . . . (*He sniffs*) Perhaps it's my little Cordelia wearing a new perfume. How now, my little darling, is it you smelling so tempting?

Renewed squeaks from the Sheep

What, still frisky? To bed with you all. Just let me close up the shelter, then it will be time to get your heads down. (*He mimes rolling a huge stone across the entrance of the cave*)

Sailor 2 (*horrified whisper*) Just look at that rock. It'd take twenty oxen to move that.

Sailor 3 Or three hundred elephants at least.

Sailor 4 I wish this stupid sheep would go away. He seems to think this is his bed.

Sailor 5 Perhaps it is. Give him a good crack. That'll teach him.

Sailor 4 Go away! Go away ...!

The Sheep butts him. He butts the Sheep. A pushing and shoving match ensues. The other Sheep gather to watch. Sailor 4 loses his temper and stamps his foot

   Go away!

The noise makes the Sheep scatter in panic. Some run to Cyclops and huddle round him for protection

Cyclops Now what's to do? What noise was that? (*He turns and sees the Crew for the first time. A long pause*) Ah ...

Ulysses (*coming forward*) Good sir, forgive us. This is not what it seems. We have craved the protection of your cave not to rob you nor harm you ...

Cyclops Who are you?

Ulysses Greeks, sir, on our way back from Troy. Ulysses is the name, general and admiral if you please.

Cyclops Ay, I've heard of you. General liar if your reputation is anything to go by.

Ulysses Sir, I must take exception to your remark. My word is as good as the next man. And when I say I mean you no harm——

Cyclops We'll see about that. So what is it you want?

Ulysses Food and drink, sir, and some shelter for my men. The gods sent us here——

Cyclops I care not a fig for your gods. As for food and drink, what fools you be if you thought you'd come here to eat and not be eaten. (*He makes a sudden movement, grabbing a dummy figure, dressed like a sailor, and whirling it over his head before sinking his teeth into it*)

Horror from the Sailors as he munches. The Sheep also draw back alarmed

   So what do you think to that, Master Ulysses? Still mean me no harm, eh?

Sheep 1 (*to Ulysses*) Please don't provoke him further, sir. He's ravenous when he's in one of these moods. Once he starts to eat, you never know when he's going to stop.

Sailor 5 But that was Knock-Knees!

Sheep 2 Who?

Sailor 5 (*shocked*) Me mate, Knock-Knees. He's eaten him!

Sheep 2 And he'll eat the rest of us if you don't shut up!

Bosun The sheep's right, son. Belt up now or we'll all be doner kebab.

Ulysses Sir, I must protest. That is one of my best midshipmen you've eaten.

Cyclops Grrrr ... rumff ... chomp ... drool ... crunch ... (*And similar noises*)
Ulysses I promised his poor mother I'd care for him like a son. Of course that was ten years ago——
Cyclops Mggguurgh—pah! (*He hurls the unfortunate Knock-Knees away and seizes another dummy to devour in the same way*) So, what are you going to do about that?
Sailors Oh, not poor Nosey Neddy! Please, sir, not poor——

Crunch. Chew. Swallow. Swallow. Poor Nosey Neddy goes the same way as Knock-Knees. The Sailors are reduced to total silence. They draw together at one end of the cave, the Sheep at the other

Sheep 1 I did warn you, didn't I? He's quite incorrigible when he's like this.
Cyclops Chew. Chew. Swallow. Swallow. (*Something sticks between his teeth and he probes to remove it*) Oink ... oink ... slobber ... slobber ... (*He swallows and hopefully manages a burp as well*) Ah, yes, Greek, no doubt about it. Fee fie foh fum, I smell the blood of a Greek man ... (*This is followed by a gigantic yawn*) What a very tasty little snack. Thank your gods for me, little man. I'll have some more for breakfast ... (*And he falls asleep*)
Sailors For breakfast? (*They eye one another suspiciously*) Who will it be? Who? ...
Sheep Lucky for us!
Sheep 3 He's quite lost his taste for mutton after that.

The Sheep settle down for the night, but the Sailors are too afraid to sleep

Sailors (*variations of*) What can we do? How can we escape?
Ulysses (*to the audience*) It was quite a dilemma for us, I can tell you. We couldn't go on providing an endless diet for him, but what could we do, trapped between that monstrous stone and his insatiable appetite? There wasn't going to be much sleep for any of us that night until we'd solved that.

The Lights narrow down to include only the Sailors with perhaps a pin-spot on the sleeping Cyclops

Sailor 6 (*after a while*) Who is this monster? Why does he look familiar? Have I seen him before? Is he the face that appears to me each night between sleeping and waking?
Sailor 7 I see him every night when I dream most deeply. I think he lives in my head for I see him most clearly when I'm afraid.
Sailor 8 My mother spoke to me of such a monster. She said if I didn't do as she said, this ... thing would come in the night and take me away. I think he had a face like this. Or something like it.
Sailor 9 I killed a man once for no good reason. Oh, I was angry or mad or drunk or perhaps all three. But ever since then this face pursues me. Sometimes I see him on the other side of the road or at the end of the street, just looking at me ...

Sailor 10 I thought I saw him once staring at me from Troy's wall. But I was wrong. It was the bloke next to me who died.

Ulysses (*to the audience*) So you see, something had to be done. Sleeping or waking, this fear had to be confronted. (*He rises and moves about the cave*) With my faithful Bosun, I searched about and found a staff of olive-wood which we sharpened and hardened in the embers of the fire.

The Bosun has joined him. The staff can be an actual prop or mimed. When the point has been hardened, they carry it to the Cyclops

(*To the audience*) You must face your fear, you see. The devils in your head must be defeated. *Now*, Bosun!

They plunge the stake into the Cyclops' single eye. A fearful sizzling sound. The monster wakes with a huge cry which wakes the Sheep and the crew. An horrendous din—drums, music, squeals from the sheep, shouts from the Sailors and from the Cyclops

Cyclops Uggowwoooh! Pogghroklumph! Wookuughrug! Help, help! They're blinding me! And after their promise to do me no harm!

Sheep (*variations of*) Baa baa baa! What's going on? Why is Father shouting so?

Sailors (*ditto*) What's to do? What has the commander done? Oh, look, look, they're attacking the monster!

Cyclops Treachery, treachery! I'll never trust your word again!

Ulysses I didn't trust you in the first place. Keep grinding, Bosun!

Bosun Ay, ay, sir!

Cyclops Aaagh! Kooopluught! Passpogght! I'll kill you ... I'll kill you! See if I don't.

Ulysses Oh, no, you won't. Now look lively, lads. Once we withdraw this pole he'll be after you!

Bosun Just one more good TWIST, sir——

Ulysses Here we go. Sorry, Cyclops, but we're only human, you see.

Sheep 3 What's going to happen to us, I wonder. After this Father will be in the most frightful mood!

Sheep 4 Just run with the others. And trust to luck.

Ulysses Here we go. Run, everybody!

The stake is withdrawn and everybody flees for safety. The Cyclops lumbers to his feet and stamps about blindly, feeling for somebody to revenge himself on. Once or twice he nearly finds a Sailor but is foiled at the last moment. Ulysses turns to the audience

This went on for the rest of the night. I may be wrong, but I think it went on the whole of the next day and night as well. Finally he settled down and started to think. So did we. How to get out of there, that was the question. We were getting jumpy. So were the sheep. If the Cyclops could have got his hands on us, he would have eaten every one of us!

Sheep 1 I don't know about you, but my stomach feels as if my throat's been cut.

Sheep 2 Me too, me too. I'm starving.

Sheep 3 Why doesn't Father roll the stone away? It's doing no good keeping us cooped up here.

Sheep 4 It's not us who's to blame. It's *them*.

Cyclops Well said, Gundrun. Well said, Nostalgia. I'll have you out in a jiffy. But as for them, all Hades will not have enough vengeance to satisfy me now. (*He fumbles his way to the big rock and rolls it away*)

Light floods in

Ulysses This was the moment the Bosun and I had been waiting for. As the sheep ran out, the Cyclops felt along the thick woolly backs of each of them. What he didn't know was that we'd tied our men *underneath* them.

Difficult to do except in mime, so as the Sheep escape into the open, the Sailors crawl out with them. Finally only Ulysses and one Sheep are left. The Cyclops feels the fleece sadly

Cyclops What is this, sweet ram. Why are you the last to leave when usually you are the first to run out to pasture? Can you be grieving for your father's eye blinded by that accursed villain? Ah, wait till I get my hands on him ...!

Ulysses escapes with the ram

Bosun Once out, we took to our heels——

Sailor 1 And made for the ship!

Sailor 2 Are you kidding? I've never run so fast in all my life!

They reach the ship and embark at once. All is a positive fury of casting off, raising sails and starting to row. Meanwhile the Cyclops has discovered he has been tricked. He takes up a position on the mountainside

Cyclops TRICKED, TRICKED BY THAT ACCURSED GREEK!

Drumbeats and thunder

  Hear me, mighty Poseidon!

Ulysses Row, boys, row!

Cyclops Girdler of the Earth, if you are indeed my father, as I believe you to be, grant that this Ulysses may never reach his home in Ithaca.

Bosun Poseidon his father? We'd forgotten that, sir.

Ulysses A regrettable oversight, Bosun, and one we may pay for.

Cyclops But if he is destined to reach his home, make sure all his comrades die and there is trouble for him in his house.

Sailor 3 Then picking up a HUGE boulder——

The drum beats faster ... faster ... faster

Sailor 4 He HURLED it into the sea!

Crash! Thunder! All the players who were recently Sheep and the corral, sweep down on the ship as waves, flowing over the vessel and crew, while the latter rock back and forth, slither and hang on for dear life. Back the waves come again and again until the huge disturbance settles

Cyclops turns and goes out

The waves lie down to rest. The Lights go to night. Soft music plays. The ship is becalmed. The crew sleep save for the Helmsman who waits patiently for the wind to come. In the meantime the vessel rocks gently. Nothing is ever completely still on a ship

SCENE 5

The Kingdom of the Winds

Helmsman Our next landfall was the floating island of Aeolia, home of Aeolus, King of the Winds, a kindly old gent with a family of six sons and six daughters who spent their days feasting and making merry. It was a proper holiday being with them, I can tell you.

Aeolus enters with his family. He is an old, old man with a floating beard of grey and a permanent sniff. The Sons and Daughters are dragging something with them which is not revealed yet

Ulysses goes to them

Ulysses Thank you, Aeolus, for your great kindness. My men and I will never forget your hospitality. My, those certainly were some feasts you gave us.

Aeolus Think nothing of it, my dear Ulysses. (*Sniff*) Next time you come, we'll really push the boat out, mark my words, ha-ha. (*Sniff*) In the meantime we have a little gift for you. (*Sniff*)

Ulysses A gift for me? How kind.

Aeolus (*to the audience*) Forgive my runny nose, but wherever I go, I'm always in a dreadful draught, you see. Well, well, (*sniff*) bring it forth, dear children, bring it forth. (*Sniff*)

The gift is revealed, a large leather bag done up at the neck with a cord

See! (*Sniff*) This will solve all your problems.

Ulysses It will? How nice! But what is it?

Aeolus (*delighted*) What is it? (*Sniff*) What is it? (*Sniff*)

Ulysses Yes, what is it? (*Sniff*)

Aeolus Wind, my dear chap. It's a bag of wind! (*Sniff*)

Ulysses Wind?

Aeolus Yes, wind. (*Sniff*) Some of each kind. There's some——

Sons —North Wind——

Aeolus —that will carry you south (*sniff*), and some——

Daughters —South Wind——

Aeolus —that will carry you north. Then there's some——

Sons —East Wind——

Aeolus —that will carry you west, and (*sniff*) some——

Daughters —West Wind——

Aeolus —that will take you the other way. Or so I am assured. So you see,

all your troubles are at an end. All you have to do is release a puff of this
or a touch of that and you'll go wherever you need. (*Sniff*)

Ulysses What a godsend, Aeolus. I can't thank you enough. This will have
us home in no time at all. (*He gives a whistle*)

Two members of the crew come down and take the bag aboard

Aeolus Now all I have to do is give you a little breeze to get you started.
Then it's up to you. (*Sniff, sniff. He makes a gesture or two*)

All Goodbye, goodbye ...

Aeolus Give our love to your dear wife ...

Helmsman And we were soon on our way.

A slight wind is heard

What a godsend indeed. It seemed all our troubles *were* over. The next
day we were actually within sight of our homeland—I could see the
washing on the lines when cursed greed took over.

Sailor 5 'Ere, lads, you know that big bag the commander brought on
board at Aeolia? What's the betting it was treasure?

Sailor 6 Treasure?

Sailor 5 Treasure.

Sailor 7 Gold and such?

Sailor 5 Absolutely.

Sailor 8 Let's take a look.

Sailor 9 Yeah, why not?

Helmsman (*greatly upset*) I mean we were actually within hand's touch of
Ithaca, when——

The bag is opened and there is a giant WHOOSH of wind

All the winds rushed out!

*Turmoil. A huge gale blows as the crew stagger and the ship is nearly capsized.
The waves come to life again and in turn storm it from the north, south, east
and west. Once again they hang on for dear life as the vessel plunges and rocks
and pitches and rolls*

Within a flash we were out to sea again and our homeland was nowhere
to be seen.

Crew Oh, no ...

Sailor 10 Goodbye, dear Ithaca. Goodbye, dear native land.

*The wind finally dies. The crew settle down once more and the Lights return
to night*

Helmsman So now we drift. I dare say after we opened that bag there wasn't
a scrap of wind left in the whole wide world.

*All movement ceases on deck. The ship has actually beached although they
don't know it yet. The Helmsman looks around in wonder*

What a night. Just right for love or witchcraft ...

SCENE 6

Circe and the Isle of Pigs

A Light appears revealing Circe the Witch, beautiful but malevolent

Circe I am Circe, daughter of Helios, mistress of all kinds of magic, good as well as evil. Once I poisoned my husband but usually I'm content to enslave men's hearts and transform their bodies. Hear me, lord Ulysses, in your sleep. Mark her and do her bidding. You and your men will stay here one whole year or even longer if I have not done with you in that time. Hear me and obey.

Ulysses stirs feverishly and wakes with a start

Ulysses What place is this?
Helmsman Place, master? We're still at sea.
Ulysses Are you blind? Look about you. Is that sand, sea? Are those trees, porpoises or whales?

The waves have come to life again and now form trees of grotesque shapes and bushes

Helmsman You're right. It's magic or else I'm dreaming. We were in deep water a moment ago.
Ulysses And may well be again if we're not careful. (*He takes up his sword and stands*) Rouse the men and stay on watch.
Circe Hear me, Ulysses, and obey.
Ulysses I'm going ashore. (*He disembarks and prowls between the trees, sword at the ready*)

The Helmsman wakes the Sailors quietly. They watch and wait for the commander's return

Sailor 1 Where do you think it is?
Sailor 2 Zeus knows. It's not Ithaca, that's for sure.
Sailor 3 If only you hadn't opened that bag of wind and let it all rush out, we'd have been there by now.
Sailor 2 Me? I like that! It weren't me. If truth be told I was the one who said we shouldn't open it!
Sailor 4 Give over. We've been through this afore. Bag of wind is a good name for you both, I'm thinking. Always talking, always sounding off.
Sailor 5 Then what place do you think it is?
Sailor 4 I think it's ... hallo, hallo ...
Others (*nervously*) What is it?
Sailor 4 That tree, I think I recognize it.
Others What?
Sailor 4 I've seen it before. Oh, no! You know where this is, don't you?
Others (*in a panic*) Where? Where?
Sailor 4 The Cyclops' island!

They scramble to their feet in alarm

All (*variations of*) Oh, no, Zeus, not again! Once was bad enough, but not twice!

Sailor 4 Yes, yes! And those animals, see! What else are they but sheep?

Some shapes can be seen moving between the trees. They grunt gently as they rootle about

There you are! Sheep!

They listen for a moment. Then Sailor 6 gives a shout of laughter

Sailor 6 That's not sheep. That's pigs!

All Pigs?

Sailor 6 Ay. Since when have you heard of sheep that grunt? It's a land entirely inhabited by porkers. We'll eat well today, lads. Roast piglets with chops and saveloys ...

Sailor 7 Chitterlings and ham!

Sailor 8 Bacon!

Sailor 9 And pig's brains!

Sailor 10 Trotters.

Sailor 1 I'll have kidneys with my bacon.

Sailor 2 I'll settle for liver. I'd go a long way for a nice slice of pig's liver. Or a cutlet. 'Ere, piggy, piggy, piggy ...

They watch as the Pigs approach and then sheer off

Helmsman I don't know though. There's something weird about those pigs.

Sailor 3 Weird?

Helmsman I can't explain it, but I get a shiver just looking at them. Just look. There's something not quite right about them. As if ...

All (*nervous*) As if ... what?

Helmsman As if they're not pigs ... but humans!

They react with horror. Ulysses appears next to them

Ulysses Quartermaster, take some men through the forest. There's a castle on the other side, dark, forbidding sort of place. Have a look round and tell me what you find.

Quartermaster Ay, ay, sir. You lot, come with me.

Sailors Oh no! Just our ruddy luck ...

They start off. The Light appears momentarily on Circe

Circe Ulysses, mark my voice and obey.

Ulysses rubs his brow as if to clear it

Ulysses I'm going to write up my log. Let me know if anything happens.

Helmsman Ay, ay, sir.

The Lights go down on the ship. We concentrate on the party of men moving through the forest

Sailor 1 I don't know. I think I must be going barmy. I can't tell if these are trees or pigs ...

Sailor 2 Or men . . .
Sailor 3 It's a sickly place and no mistake.
Sailor 4 If you ask me, I'd rather be back on the Cyclops' island.
Sailor 1 Are you there, Nobby? Nobby, are you there?

Sailor 2 gives a grunt

Answer can't you?

Man 2 gives another grunt. Man 1 takes a look and leaps in astonishment

'Struth, there's one of them pigs right next to me!
Sailor 2 Don't be an idiot, it's me. Nobby!
Sailor 1 But you're a . . . pig!
Sailor 3 So are you!
Sailor 4 And you!
Quartermaster Oh, Zeus, oh, Hades. We're all pigs!

Circe is moving among them now. They drop on all fours and grunt as they move about

Circe You're all pigs. All the men on this island are pigs, save Ulysses, whom I am preserving for reasons of my own.
Quartermaster Zeus help us all!
Circe In this place Zeus holds no sway. I am Circe and my magic rules this island with spells and witchcraft. Pigs you are and pigs you'll stay until I change my mind.
Sailor 1 There's the castle the commander mentioned. Grunt, grunt.
Sailor 2 It looks more like a prison, grunt, grunt.
Sailor 3 Or a gigantic pigsty, oink, oink.
Circe All pigs and trees away! Go, seek your acorns elsewhere!

All trees and Pigs clear to another part and watch

Come, Ulysses, you heard my voice. Obey.

Ulysses moves towards her

Ulysses You've done this? All my men and these others, turned to pigs! But why? Do you hate men so?
Circe Not hate. Simply show them what they are. Ill-formed, gross by nature, lacking feeling and insight. Suitors, shipwrecked sailors, all pigs with pigs' heads and bristles. Only their minds stay untouched except they remember nothing. Nothing of who they are or where they came from.
Ulysses And I? Why have you spared me? O Zeus, if you cannot save my men, then make me one of them!
Circe Not until I give the word. (*She moves away*) Come to my palace. There's feasting for us. For these others, acorns and berries and plenty of mud to wallow in.

Ulysses is about to follow when

A ragged Peasant approaches, hooded and clutching a staff

Peasant Ulysses, listen to me, but do not turn your head. Don't show Circe I am here.

Ulysses (*standing with his back to him*) Who are you?

Peasant Hermes, the Giant Killer. When you feel yourself threatened—and threaten you she will—draw your sword and rush on her as if you mean to kill her. To mollify you, she'll give you a drink filled with drugs, hoping to make you like these other men. But before you drink, drop this herb into the wine. It is rightly called *moly* and that will save you from her spell.

Ulysses How will I know when to do this?

Peasant You will know. Go now and the gods go with you. (*He brushes against Ulysses and in so doing passes him the herb—a white flower with a black root*)

He leaves as quietly as he came

Circe (*returning to him*) Now we are home! (*She makes a gesture*)

Warm Lights come up to change the setting into an interior. Some of the others come forward with a carpet and cushions, bowls of fruits and wine. The Pigs stay oinking at the door, but the girls lead Ulysses forward and serve him with refreshment. Music plays

Now the time is ripe for explanations. You are to stay with me for all time and be my husband. Come, I am not ugly and I have more power in my one hand than you and all your fellow kings combined. Come, do not seek to argue. This is not a wish, but a command.

Ulysses And if I disobey?

Circe You've seen what has happened to the others. If you don't obey, you'll be the same.

Ulysses Then you're right, *the time is ripe!* (*He seizes up his sword and makes as if to kill her*) Say your farewells, witch, for your last spell has been cast!

Circe screams

Circe No, Ulysses, no! Do not kill me. I'll spare you if you agree to marry me. Here, take this wine. It will seal our agreement and help to mollify you.

Ulysses laughs, takes the wine, but in turning away, drops the flower into it. Then he drinks. Circe watches in triumph

You fool! All you men are so easily tricked! Who'd have such an imbecile for a husband? Go, pig, drop on all fours and join your fellows in the mud. I'll teach you to reject me.

Ulysses No, Circe, you are the fool. Your spell has no effect on me. See I am still on two legs and my head has no bristles. What is more I remember who I am and where I came from.

Circe Hermes! Hermes did this for you!

Ulysses Does it matter? Now I am free and so are my men.

Circe No, only I can free them and you have not obeyed my conditions. Stay with me a month, a year, Ulysses. Marry me and haul your ship

ashore. Make your home with me without complaint and I'll free your
men.

Ulysses You swear this?

Circe I swear.

*Ulysses ponders this and then he nods. The Pigs stand and raise a cheer of
relief. The Lights go down on the central feast and the Sailors move forward*

Quartermaster We were content to stay a year. Truth to tell, we were fed
up with all that rowing and getting nowhere and we had to fill in the time
somehow. In no time at all we were restored to normal with feasting and
enjoyment in abundance. What the commander and that witch got up to,
I wouldn't like to ask, but we had no complaints for twelve months, I
can tell you.

Sailor But all good things must come to an end. Indeed everything comes
to an end if you wait long enough.

Circe moves forward and addresses him

Circe The time has come for you to make another departure. This time
Poseidon orders you to sail to the very Halls of Hades, the Kingdom of
the Dead itself. Here you are to consult the soul of the dead prophet
Tiresias and debate the wishes of those who died long ago.

Sailor I?

Circe You are to be Ulysses now.

Ulysses II hands over the beard and calls to the others

Ulysses II Come, we'll await our commander at the ship.

*The Sailors move to the ship accompanied by many of the land party. They
take their farewells and embark. Meanwhile . . .*

Ulysses III But who is to guide us to Hell? Nobody has ever gone that way
and returned.

Hermes the Peasant returns. Now he throws back his hood to reveal his face

Hermes Ulysses of the Nimble Wits, set your mast and spread your sail.
The North Wind will do the rest. When you reach Persephone's Grove,
beach your ship and dig a trench a cubit long and a cubit wide. Around
this trench, pour offerings to all the dead, first with honey mixed with
milk, then with sweet wine and last of all with water. Over this sprinkle
white barley and begin your prayers to the helpless dead. When you've
finished, sacrifice a young ram and a black ewe. Then the dead will appear.
But mark this, *do not speak to them* until Tiresias appears. One word
before its time will bring your downfall. Go now and keep your wits
about you.

Ulysses Good Hermes, I obey.

Circe Farewell, Ulysses, may your journey make good sailing.

Ulysses Lady, I go and for your hospitality I salute you. (*He takes up his
position on the ship*) Come, we sail for the Land of the Dead.

They cast off

Those on shore wave and slowly retreat to prepare for the next scene

Sailor 1 The North Wind blows.

Ulysses Then set sail and say your prayers. When we see land again, it will be a damnable place.

The Lights go down with a rush, leaving only a small spot on Ulysses

SCENE 7

The Land of the Dead

Ulysses O Father Zeus, give me the strength to contend. Help me not to be rash and impulsive. Too often I act without thinking. Give me patience now and courage. Many times I've survived ordeal by fire and steel. I've conquered cities and demi-gods, but I have never confronted an army of the dead. Spare me my soul, O Zeus, leave me that which is special to everyone.

Ghostly music. The sound of water dripping

Sailor 1 (*afraid*) All is grown dark ...
Sailor 2 We are sailing down a long tunnel, I think ...
Sailor 3 It's a cavern large as any city. All stone ...
Ulysses Take soundings. We don't want to go aground here.
Sailor 4 By the mark five ... four ...
Sailor 5 Are we under the earth?
Sailor 6 Do the dead really live here? It is a cheerless place ...
Sailor 4 By the mark three ...
Sailor 7 Must we also come here one day, spend all eternity in a place like this?
Sailor 4 By the mark two ... one ..

The ship gives a faint judder. Ulysses leaps ashore

Ulysses (*briskly*) Come, dig the trench as Hermes ordered and prepare the sacrifices. And be of strong heart. Remember you are here by order of the gods. Follow their directions and you'll come to no harm.

They proceed with the mime of the digging

Now the three offerings—honey and milk, sweet wine and ... clear water.

This is done

And the white barley. Now prepare the ram and the ewe while I say our prayer to almighty Zeus. "Great god, we have come as you bade us. Be pleased with our sacrifice to you and help us achieve the purpose of our visit. I, Ulysses, son of royal Laertes, called the Schemer and the Nimble-Witted, say these things to you. Hear us as we seek sanction and grant that no word fall from us that is unfit for the present need." (*He does obeisance and then turns to his men*) Now the sacrifices. Let the blood run into the trench. "See, Father Zeus, the bright red blood of the offerings, neither tainted nor diluted. All is as was ordered." Now we wait ...

The Sailors retreat apprehensively. A slight wind moans and echoes through the cave. Then the moaning rises slightly in volume

Grey Ghosts appear from the dark

The Sailors tremble. Even Ulysses is far from happy

What, so soon? Great Zeus, you waste no time. Very well then. Let them come. (*To his men*) But remember, speak to no-one. Tiresias will come when he is ready. Until then use only your eyes, not your tongues.

The Ghosts advance slowly. The moaning begins to take form—"Ulysses, Ulysses ..." is what we hear most. This develops into variations of "Save us ... help us ... lead us from this place". They cluster round him and begin to paw at him gently, stroking his face and taking hold of his clothes. He is appalled and tries to disengage himself

Ulysses Take them away ... take them away!
Ulysses II Do not speak to them, whatever you do!
Ulysses I He must, he must! Order them to go, Ulysses!
Ulysses I dare not! The god commanded!
Ulysses II He must not. Be calm, Ulysses, they cannot harm you!

Some of the Spirits now move along the crew and repeat their appeals to the Sailors who are terrified of the contact

Sailors (*variations of*) Take them way, Zeus! Away, foul spirits! Hermes, protect us! Save us, almighty Achilles!
Sailor 8 Oh, God, I see my brother. I must speak to him!
Others No, you mustn't!
Sailor 8 I must, I must! Lelex, it is I, your brother!

Instantly he goes down as the Spirits claim him

Others Gag him! Stop him!
Others Too late!
Sailor 8 Help me ...
Others Too late. He's lost.
Ulysses O Zeus, save us! Tiresias, come!

A drum beats, slow and inexorable. The Spirits break away and cower back. At the far end of the acting area—as far off as possible—a Light begins to glow. Ulysses drops to his knees. The Sailors follow suit

Two macabre Attendants appear, perhaps dressed in black body-tights painted with white skeletons or as Bull Dancers with bull-masks surmounted by great golden horns. Tiresias follows, a very old man, blind, led by a Child. They approach slowly

Everybody waits. Finally, when they are in position, the old man speaks

Tiresias I am called. Who speaks?

Ulysses It is I, great prophet. Ulysses, son of royal Laertes. I called to you.

Tiresias Ulysses? Why did you call? Surely you know the dead have no right of appeal? Once here you are condemned to your fate, whatever it is.

Ulysses Mighty seer, beloved of the gods, know that I was sent here by Hermes, messenger of Zeus, to seek your aid in my return home.

Tiresias Ah, I remember now. You offended Poseidon mightily by destroying Troy. That was your first crime. Then you blinded his son, the Cyclops, that was your second. Small wonder now you travel in circles unable to reach Ithaca.

Ulysses It's true none can antagonize the gods with impunity, but it's equally true we have always spent many years appeasing Poseidon's anger. Surely our trial is near an end. Is that not why we were sent to consult you?

Tiresias Alas for you, son of Laertes, there is nothing I can do to lessen the edict of a god. All I can do is warn you of the dangers still ahead. That is the limit of my power. Nor can I even tell you of the order in which they'll come. Leaving here you will come to the Land of the Sacred Cattle. Beware! These must not be hurt in any way. To do so will be to risk total destruction for you and your crew. In time you must also face the twin threats of the great rocks Scylla and Charybdis which will seek to pull you first one way, and then the other, to your deaths. Avoid both, steer always for the middle way in all things. Sometime too you will be tempted to indulgence in the songs of the Sirens. Take heed you hear them not. Stuff your ears with beeswax and have your crew bind you to your mast lest you follow where the Sirens beckon. All this and more must you face before you come home, and even then—if you should reach that shore— you will find all in turmoil. For your kingdom is threatened by many rivals, while your grieving wife, Penelope, has all but given up hope of seeing you again.

Ulysses Oh, gods, is there no light for me at all?

Tiresias There is light for all men if they do as their destiny tells them. But it is of your end I wish to speak. If you should survive all this and all voyages and all returns having been made, to win respite from the gods, you must take an oar, an ordinary rowing oar, and carry it to the furthest country you can find—so far from the ocean that the inhabitants will not know what it is you carry—and there bury the instrument and make sacrifices to Poseidon. Only then will you know your voyage is finally at an end and that you have appeased the gods. And only then will you find your reconciliation and enjoy your old age.

Ulysses Alas, so far off a time?

Tiresias So far, and yet no longer than it takes a god to blink his eye. Come, you must be gone now. I have spoken. There is no more.

Ulysses But, great lord, is there no way you can shorten our journey? We are a valiant crew and god-fearing!

Tiresias There is no more. It is finished.

He gestures to his Attendants and they begin their retreat to the shadows

Ulysses No! Stay, honoured spirit. There must be more. A horrible and pernacious voyage we made to reach you. Can you give no more comfort than this?
Tiresias No more.
Ulysses Then I'll follow you and force it from you!

He makes as if to follow. The Sailors make a move to stop him

Ulysses II Seize him! Hold him! Courage, Ulysses!
Sailor 1 Please, my lord, I beg you! Do not follow him or we'll all be lost.

They overpower Ulysses

The Lights fade on Tiresias and his Attendants

The other spirits start to leave

Ulysses O gods, I think I see my mother and my sisters! Speak to me! Say something, Mother. Can you not see me? And my sisters, have you forgotten me so soon? Is that the truth of being dead, that you forget the living before we forget you?
Ulysses I Come, bring him to the ship.
Ulysses And all my dead companions—Agamemnon and great Achilles, Ajax and Patroclus, Iacchus and Diomedes, old Melaneus and his son Lynchus—so many, many ... Speak! Have you no word for me? None of you? (*In despair*) Nothing?
Ulysses II To the ship. We must return to the land of the living.

They carry him to the ship and set sail once more

The Spirits have gone

The Lights return and the atmosphere grows cheerful once more. Ulysses II takes over until the present commander has recovered

Ulysses II (*to the audience*) The honoured Tiresias had told us some of the trials we still had to face, but even he hadn't known the order in which they'd come. We were not left long in ignorance.

SCENE 8

Back to the Land of the Living

A slight wind rises. Soft seductive music comes and goes as if wafted on the wind; no specific theme, a wordless song perhaps. Ulysses stirs

Ulysses That music ... it promises salvation. Where does it come from?
Sailor 2 (*pointing*) Over there.
Sailor 3 No. (*Pointing another way*) Over there.
Sailor 4 I think it's in the air above us.
Ulysses No, we must follow it. Helmsman, steer that course.
Helmsman Ay, ay, sir.

They sail on contented for a while. Then the music returns more loudly from another direction

Sailor 2 There! I said it was *that* way.
Sailor 5 You said it was the other way.
Sailor 4 I knew it was from the air above us.
Sailor 6 How can that be, stupid?
Sailor 4 (*a shrug*) Perhaps the gods sent it.
Ulysses (*remembering*) The gods? Did Tiresias not say——?

The music ceases abruptly

Sailor 7 There, now it's gone.

They look round as if to find it

Sailor 8 No, I think it's coming from over there.
Sailor 9 No, it's stopped.

It reappears. Louder

Sailor 10 No, there it is again. (*Pointing*) From over there.
Ulysses Helmsman, steer that way. Follow the music!
Sailor 1 No, sir, the other way.
Sailor 2 Listen, women singing ...
Sailor 3 Beautiful ...
Sailor 4 Seductive. Makes me think of my wife.
Sailor 5 (*scornful*) Your wife? You should be so lucky.
Helmsman Rocks ahoy! (*He tries to change course*)
Ulysses Why are you changing course? Did I give the order?
Helmsman Rocks, commander. We are being lured to the rocks!
Sailor 6 It's the song of the Sirens! Sir, remember what Tiresias said!
Sailor 7 Beeswax! We must stuff his ears with beeswax!
Sailor 8 And tie him to the mast!

The others take up the cry

Ulysses Fools, let me go! *That* is the course for Ithaca!
Sailors (*variations of*) Bind him to the mast. Master, it's what Tiresias said.
Ulysses Fools, let me go! Am I not the commander of the ship?
Sailor 9 I've the beeswax!
Sailor 10 And I've the rope!

Ulysses is bound to the mast and his ears are plugged with wax. The ship begins to tip and tilt—not too much yet, that comes later—as the Helmsman struggles to keep on course. Ulysses shouts above the Sirens' song

Ulysses You are right, you are right! What a fool I am! It is the song of the Sirens. Hold to your old course, Helmsman! Zeus, forgive me! I nearly led them to their death, being as impulsive as ever!

The wind increases

One of the Sirens appears in a single spotlight

Siren Draw near, Ulysses. No seaman ever passed his ship beyond our rocks without listening to our wisdom. We know what you have suffered. Listen to our message and we will bring you peace and consolation.
Ulysses (*despairing*) I can still hear her. More wax!
Helmsman Master, I am helpless against her! What shall I do?
Ulysses Wax for the helmsman also! Help him to steer us to safety! Then all use the wax! All! All!

The Sailors race to help the Helmsman. The Siren calls again. They plug their ears with wax

Siren Do not struggle against us, Ulysses. Give in to temptation. That is the best way to get rid of it.
Ulysses (*a big roar*) Row! Take up the oars and row!

They obey. Music of another kind vies with the first

Faster, harder! Take us away from these seductive rocks!
Siren Come, Ulysses ...
Bosun (*giving the rowing rate*) Faster, lads, faster. One ... two ... one ... two ... one ... two ... (*Using gestures*)
Sailor 1 What do you think they would do?
Sailor 2 (*can't hear*) Eh?
Sailor 1 What do you think they'd do if they got us? (*Happily*) I can just imagine ...

They row harder. The Light fades on the Siren. After a while the music begins to fade. The Bosun takes the wax from his ears and listens. He goes to Ulysses

Bosun Beg to report, sir, no sirens.
Ulysses WHAT?
Bosun (*shouting*) NO SIRENS! ALL——

Ulysses takes the wax from his ears. Bosun's voice fades away

—gone ...
Ulysses Thank Zeus. That was a close thing.
Bosun Ay, that it was. Now then, lads, look lively. Untie the commander.

They do so during the following

Sailor 1 Here, Lofty, what d'you think they would have done?
Sailor 2 Who?
Sailor 1 Them Sirens, of course. What d'you think they would have done?
Sailor 3 Sucked your brains out, of course. What d'you think?
Sailor 1 No kidding?
Sailor 4 If they could find any brains, that is!

Laughter

Ulysses Hallo, what's that roaring?
Bosun Roaring?
Ulysses Roaring. (*Jumpy*) What challenge is this?

We can hear it now. The sound of racing water. The wind rises

Helmsman Channel ahead, sir.
Sailor 5 And rocks!
Sailor 6 Rocks!!
Ulysses Scylla and Charybdis! Helmsman, steer the middle course!
Helmsman (*battling with the steering oar*) Easier said than done!

Suddenly the uproar is deafening—wind, sea and the cries of the men. The rest of the cast now take up two sides and call out, "This way ... this way" trying to draw the ship to them. Also the sea grows considerably rougher than any we've seen until now. Remember this should not call for faster movement from the crew as the decks pitches and rolls, but slower and deeper action

Bosun Keep rowing. Row, row! Helmsman, watch out. (*Pointing*) Whirlpools!

The cast on that side have formed themselves into circles or spirals that swirl closer and closer to the ship, while on the other side ...

Quartermaster Look, tidal waves!

The other half have formed groups that race upon the ship

Ulysses Helmsman, keep to the middle path.
Helmsman Sir, I can't. The pull is too strong, first one way and then the other.
Ulysses (*to the crew*) Help him! All hands to the tiller!

Some manage to reach the steering oar and lend their weight to holding it straight. But most of them have their time cut out trying to retain their balance. Their desperate struggles should now show us the vessel is rolling heavily from side to side and with each roll hurling the Sailors from one side to the other. Again, remember, mountainous seas are not quicker but deeper, and the movement more monumental. So huge does this rise and fall become that one of the sailors finds himself sliding overboard

Sailor Help! Help!

Panic measures to rescue him. All the time the wind howls, the ship rolls and pitches and the sea on either side advances or withdraws or breaks right over the deck, swamping everything. Music and drums add to the pandemonium while the Lights rise and fall. Now, as the channel appears to grow more narrow, the waves sweep closer and even try to drag the Sailors from the ship, first one side and then the other

Waves I SCYLLA!
Waves II CHARYBDIS!
Waves I SCYLLA!
Waves II CHARYBDIS!

Some of the Sailors are lost in the confusion and disappear in a tangle of arms and legs. Then both halves break over the ship, intermingle and change sides to race round and round it so that it appears to be caught in a gigantic whirlpool. Surely now it must sink

Ulysses Zeus, save us!

On cue the waves "explode" upwards with a giant leap and shout ... and slowly subside. The surviving Sailors shut their eyes expecting the worst, until one cries out

Sailor Thank the gods, we're through!

Indeed they are. The wind dies down

The waves back off and are left behind

The Sailors collapse on the deck in huge relief. Ulysses manages to raise his arms to the sky

Ulysses Great Zeus, Father Zeus, thank you. Thank you.

Poseidon speaks unseen

Poseidon (*on amplifier*) Don't give thanks too soon, Ulysses. It's not over yet.

Ulysses hasn't the strength to reply. The Sailors count the number lost

Sailor 1 So many gone ...
Sailor 2 Half our number ...
Sailor 3 So many?
Sailor 4 Maybe more.
Sailor 5 Will any of us survive to reach home, I wonder.
Sailor 6 Perhaps the drowned are the lucky ones. What worse things has Poseidon in store for us, I ask myself.
Bosun Who knows, lad? But one thing's certain. He won't tell. Get moving then. Let's get shipshape.
Ulysses Thank you, Bosun. We're winning through. Each day we're getting stronger and more courageous. So take up your oars again, I beseech you, and let us advance further down the years. We'll get home, I promise you.

The Survivors settle down to row steadily but quietly. Once again the Lights narrow down on Ulysses. Alone he shows he is not as confident as he sounded

SCENE 9

The Sacred Cattle of the Sun

Ulysses Do they believe me? Do *I* believe me? Each night I say my prayers, "Zeus, bring us safely home", but I've lost all sense of time. Sometimes it seems we've travelled all our lives and sometimes it feels we must continue for all eternity. "O Father Zeus, let it end. We are so tired of wandering." When I'm not speaking to the gods, I'm thinking of my poor wife Penelope and my son Telemachus. There's trouble at home, Tiresias warned me, with rivals casting envious looks at my kingdom. What does my wife think of this, and my son, how does he view these would-be fathers? Has he forgotten me by now? He was only a child when I left. Now he's almost a man. Don't forget me, Telemachus, the little you know of me. "O Zeus, take us home. Soon." (*He lies down to sleep*)

A long pause

Sailor 1 Ye gods, I'm starving!
Sailor 2 I could eat a sheep.
Sailor 3 A horse.
Sailor 4 An ox.

One of the Sun Cattle speaks from just out of sight. The Lights come up to day

Girl 1 (*off*) Here they come. Let's make ready.
Girl 2 (*off*) Did you hear what they said? One wants to eat an ox!
Girl 1 (*off*) I heard. They'll soon get their wish.
Girl 2 (*off*) The Sun-god won't be pleased.
Girl 1 (*off*) But Poseidon will be delighted.

The crew has stopped rowing. Now they sit sadly on the deck, their bodies still swaying to the movement of the ship

Sailor 1 I tell you I'm starving!
Sailor 2 You told us that already.
Sailor 3 I could eat a couple of sheep!
Sailor 4 Five horses!
Sailor 5 Three oxen!

An ox bellows off stage, followed by another and another

Sailor 2 Did you hear that?
Sailor 3 A sheep?
Sailor 2 No, you fool—
Sailor 4 Not a horse?
Sailor 2 Blithering idiot. An ox ...
Sailor 5 Three oxen!
Sailor 1 Where?
Sailor 2 There. On that narrow strip of land. See?
Sailor 3 More than three ...
All Enough for all of us!

The Sun Cattle appear. They walk slowly and sedately, not on all fours, but upright, with their arms curled above their heads like giant horns. Soft music plays. They are quite obviously magic beasts

The Sailors are fascinated

Sailor 1 Cor! Look at that!
Sailor 2 Fantastic!
Sailor 3 Too good to eat!
Sailor 4 Don't you believe it. (*Rubbing his tummy*) Yum-yum.

Sailor 1 Bags I the first one.
Sailor 2 Bags I the second.
Sailor 3 I'll take the rest.
Sailor 1 Come on, you lot. Let's hunt them before Ulysses wakes. We'll surprise him with a cooked breakfast.
Sailor 2 He'll be surprised all right.

They take their spears and slip ashore. Cautiously and with great skill they stalk the Cattle, making use of whatever cover they can find and "freezing" when the sacred beasts turn

Girl 1 They think we can't see them.
Girl 2 That's the idea.
Girl 3 Lord, what fools these mortals be.
Girl 4 The only trouble is . . .
Others What?
Girl 4 One of us will have to make the ultimate sacrifice.
Girl 1 That's the luck of the draw.
Girl 2 And Poseidon's wishes.

The Sailors are lying on their tummies looking down at the Sun Cattle who are lowering their heads to drink at a stream

Sailor 1 There, that first one.
Sailor 2 The second one looks better.
Sailor 3 What's it matter? Just get one. Any one! I'm bloody famished!
Sailor 1 All right. Let's go then!

They race down on the herd, separate one from the others and kill her quickly

Girl 1 Just my luck. It's always the same. God bless Poseidon and all his little ones. Amen. (*She dies*)
Sailor 1 Now carry her back to the ship.
Sailor 2 We'd better make a sacrifice.
Sailor 3 There's no barley. Anyway I'm hungry.
Sailor 4 Can't we eat her first and sacrifice later?
Sailor 1 Are we going to roast her?
Sailor 2 No, bake her!
Sailor 3 Fry her with chips! What's it matter? Let's just get on with it!

They mime all this. As they settle down to eat Ulysses wakes

Ulysses (*sniffing*) What sweet smells are these? Oh, ye gods, how my mouth waters. Roast beef? It must be a banquet.

He glances up to see some of the Sun Cattle posed on a rock looking very impressive indeed

Hell's Harpies! What are they up to? (*He races to the men*) You dolts, dizzards, simpletons and boobies! Do you realize what you've done?
Sailor 1 Hallo, commander, like a bite?
Ulysses Rabbit-brain, they are the Sun Cattle, Hyperion's prize herd!
Sailor 2 The Sun Cattle?

Sailor 3 Hyperion's *what*?
Sailor 4 Oh, no!
Ulysses You heard!
Sailor 5 What Tiresias said?
Ulysses Exactly! "Leave them untouched," he said. "Hurt them and you'll risk total destruction." (*Falling on his knees*) O Zeus, forgive us!
All (*following suit*) Forgive us.
Ulysses They didn't know what they did.
All We didn't know, we didn't know.

A growl of thunder in the distance

Sailor 1 Did you hear that? His revenge is starting already.
Sailor 2 In any case we can't eat this meat. See, it's rotten! Maggots and worms ...
Sailor 3 Ugh, that's witchcraft! We'd better get out of here.
Ulysses Quick, back to the ship before Poseidon hears!

They race back to the ship

Girl 2 A neat job well done. There might even be a nice little bonus in it for us.

Mighty pleased with themselves the Sun Cattle leave

The Sailors start to row, quickly at first, but then settling into a quiet rhythm. The rowing music returns

Crew   O—eeoh O!
                                  O—eeoh O! ...

They keep this up in the background

Ulysses I (*to the audience*) We rowed all that day and the next.
Ulysses II It seemed Poseidon had not noticed our misdemeanour.
Ulysses I Then a sombre cloud appeared above the ship, darkening the sea with its shadow.
Ulysses II And a new wind arose from the west.
Sailor 1 (*looking up*) They say it's always darkest before the storm.
Sailor 2 Dawn, you idiot, dawn. It's always darkest before the *dawn*.
Sailor 1 Well, it looks like a storm to me.

The music breaks off as they stop their rowing and look about them

The rest of the cast who have been waves, Sailors, magic Cattle and so on, can now be seen crouching in the shadows around the ship. Poseidon appears in his spotlight high up

The Sailors see him

Sailor Hey-up, there's trouble.
Ulysses Take cover. It's Poseidon's revenge!

Poseidon mimes whirling a sling-shot over his head ... faster ... faster—and

*releases it. A shrill whine as it passes through the air. Then as it strikes the
ship, the cast gathered in the dark, explode upwards with a great cry*

All POW!!

Ulysses I The thunderbolt struck the mast of the ship, bringing it down.

Ulysses II It snapped as it fell, breaking the helmsman's neck and bringing
all the rigging with it.

*On the ship all is confusion. The waves storm the vessel, sweeping all before
them. As we have had so much noise up to now, it might be interesting to play
as much of this as possible in silence, but with BIG movement giving us the
drama. Slow-motion is also a possibility. Factually the Helmsman collapses
and is washed overboard. One by one all the other Sailors are also washed off
the ship, carried away by the others whom they then join, first swimming, then
drowning. Ulysses alone remains on the sinking ship*

Ulysses I The whole ship reeled to the force of the thunderbolt and then
began to sink.

Ulysses II All my men were flung overboard to drown. There'd be no
homecoming for them after all.

Ulysses I My heart broke for them. So much courage, so much loyalty gone
for nothing.

Ulysses II Within an instant I was alone.

Ulysses I managed to lash two spars together and clung to them——

Ulysses II —as the sea washed over all and the ship disappeared beneath
the waves.

*The sea picks Ulysses up and sweeps him bodily around the acting area. Ulysses
I and II now join in with the mass action. The wind and the sound of the storm
now return with music. The Lights which have gone dark during the storm give
us lightning from time to time. The action continues on as big a scale as
possible, so that Ulysses is swept from one end to the other, now held up high,
then plunged low and submerged. Then slowly the movement subsides. The
Lights start to return. The thunder and wind finally cease. Soft, beguiling
music emerges. The waves bring Ulysses to rest in the centre of the acting area
and then retreat to the perimeter to crouch and watch. Everything stills.
Ulysses lies motionless*

Ulysses I For nine days I was washed about by the heedless sea.

Ulysses II Nine days of drifting followed by a death-like state.

Ulysses I All my companions were gone.

Ulysses II And I was totally alone at the mercy of the gods.

Ulysses I Then on the tenth day I was washed up on a distant shore, all
golden sand and coral.

Ulysses II It was the island of the nymph Calypso. Thickets of alder, black
poplar and cypress crowded the beach. Parsley and irises grew in a nearby
meadow. Here he was left to recover. And here let us leave him for a
while ...

The rest of the cast rise and leave quietly

Ulysses remains alone and unconscious for a long while as the mirror-ball returns briefly filling the theatre with stars. Then all the Lights go down to darkness

BLACK-OUT

ACT II

Before the house lights go down, a strange group starts assembling in the acting area. The males wear suits and ties and the females dresses or street coats and hats. Hats? Preferably the style should be of the thirties, forties or early fifties, if possible nothing of today. And no jeans. These are the Gods and Goddesses gathering for a meeting

There are as many as the director thinks necessary. Some carry brief-cases (rather battered from over-use) or files of documents. All look harassed and over-worked. They could be the managerial staff of some smallish industrial concern. We certainly would not expect them to be deities and the revelation should come as a surprise to the audience when they learn it. During the intermission, several benches or straight chairs have been brought in and a table set for the Chairman laid with a carafe of water, a tumbler, notebooks and a small handbell.

While waiting to start, the divinities gather in small groups, talk in low voices, discuss their notes, sharpen their pencils, polish their spectacles or sort their papers. They break off as . . .

Another of their number, Poseidon, enters, possibly accompanied by one or two Attendants. Unlike the others he is dressed in his full regalia and still carries his trident

His appearance causes a sharp reaction. While showing him respect, the others try to ignore him as much as possible

A gong sounds off stage and Zeus enters hurriedly. As before he is dressed in a nondescript suit and is followed by his Secretary carrying a huge pile of files which continually threatens to drop from her arms

The house lights finally go down

SCENE 1

The Conference

Zeus (*hurrying to his place*) Let's get on with it then. The whole blasted affair's taken up far too much time as it is. Well, come on, come on, to your places! (*He sits at the table and tinkles the handbell*) If you're not ready now, you never will be.

The Secretary sits beside him and tries to arrange her papers. The others find places for themselves and sit. Except for Poseidon. He remains standing at the far end, an imposing over-dignified figure

Well, ladies and gentlemen—er, sons and daughters—I daresay you'll be wondering what all the fuss is about. To tell the truth, so am I. All this hoo-ha just for one person.

Athene (*standing*) Not just *any* person, Father. (*She breaks off in apology*) I'm sorry, *Mr Chairman* ... but somebody fairly special. (*She sits again in some embarrassment. Now we see she is wearing a coat over her white dress*)

Zeus (*with a glare at Athene*) As I was saying, lass, all this fuss just for one person. Now what's his name again this ...?

Secretary Odysseus.

Zeus No, no, his other name!

Athene Ulysses.

Zeus That's him, this Ulysses. Him of the Nimble Wits as he likes to call himself. Son of royal Laertes. Or so he says.

Poseidon Ha!

Zeus That'll do from you, Poseidon. You'll speak when you're spoken to and not before. And while we're about it, you ought to know you've mightily offended the dignity of this Court turning up here like that in your working clothes.

Agreement from the others. Poseidon bridles

Oh, I've no doubt you've got your reasons——

Poseidon I've had to come straight from the office——

Zeus So have we all, but look at us. If we could manage a decent change of clothing, so could you. Now where were we?

Secretary Ulysses.

Zeus That's the chap. Well, we all know about him. He wants to go home again. (*A little joke*) Just like the rest of us, I daresay. (*Sharply*) Wake up, Apollo!

Apollo (*with a start*) Sorry, Father.

Zeus Five years he's been wandering now——

Secretary Seven.

Athene Ten.

Zeus Are you sure? (*To Secretary*) Is Athene sure?

Secretary (*flustered*) There is some doubt ...

Athene No doubt at all. Ten.

Secretary Well, there was three years before Calypso——

Athene And seven years there. Ten.

Zeus Is that so? Seven with Calypso? Not bad going, eh?

Poseidon (*booming*) Still not long enough if you ask me.

Zeus As it happens, nobody is asking you. Well, not right off, that is. Ten, eh? Well, it is a long time, but what we've got to decide, gods and goddesses, is IS IT ENOUGH?

Poseidon and **Some** No!

Others Yes!

Zeus Yes, well, I can see you all have your own opinions but that's what we've got to decide. Now I know you've all had a long day at the office and there's many more important worries to take home with you, but what my daughter here—the great goddess Athene—has asked us to decide once and for all is—*wake up, Apollo!*——

Apollo Er ... er ...

Zeus —whether this ... this——

Secretary Ulysses.

Zeus —has had enough? Well now, daughter, speak.

Athene (*rising*) Thank you, Mr Chairman, great Zeus, God of Gods, Lord of the Universe, mighty Warrior and Prince, Son of Cronos, Gatherer of the Clouds——

Poseidon All right, all right, just get on with it.

Zeus Oh, no you don't. We'll have the proper procedure if you don't mind. Go on, lass.

Athene Creator of Day and Night, Emperor of the Land and Sky, King of the Rocks and Stars, Suzerain of the Mountains and so on and so on and so on.

Poseidon But not god of the sea! That's my domain!

Zeus Nobody said I was. Right, Athene, present your case.

Athene As your lordship knows, this Ulysses first met with my disapproval over his behaviour in Troy. Before the last fighting started, he entered into a contract with me whereby he swore to spare all the loyal inhabitants of the city when the victory came as well as respecting all its sacred monuments and shrines. But when the time came——

God Yes, yes, we know all that!

Goddess Let 'er finish!

Uproar

Zeus Order! Order! (*He rings the little bell*)

Athene —when the time came, he led the slaughter and vandalism himself.

God 1 Shame!

God 2 Oh, no, he didn't.

Others Oh yes, he did!

Athene For which he later apologized and was punished.

Poseidon But not enough! The man's an inveterate liar!

Athene That's a matter of opinion. My right honourable lord there, my gracious uncle Poseidon——

Poseidon Well, let's have all *my* rank and titles then.

Athene —agreed with me the punishment should be a severe one seeing that Troy had been one of his favourite possessions——

Poseidon A lovely spot, right on the sea. Can't go there now. Quite ruined.

Athene —and ten years, we decided, should be the sentence for this mighty insult. That is ten years of wandering before he could come home to his loving wife and son.

Some Ten years? A mere pittance? Not nearly long enough ... (*etc.*)

Others Ten years? Utterly barbaric. Far too long! These judges, nothing but sadists. How would you like it ... (*etc.*)

Zeus Order, order!

Order is restored

Athene With all this I concurred, but now those ten years are up.
Poseidon No!
Athene Yes!
Zeus Are you sure? Not five?
Secretary Seven!
Athene Ten! And I want the order of this House to make it clear the sentence has been served and he can return home to Ithaca without delay.
Zeus Without delay? That's a good one. He didn't seem to mind hanging about with Calypso for seven of them.
Athene That's beside the point!
Zeus Some point. I wouldn't mind a bit of it myself. (*To Secretary*) When did I last visit Calypso?
Poseidon It's all a nonsense! If he'd really wanted to get home, he would have tried before now! A two-faced liar.

Uproar

Athene Not with you opposing him he couldn't.
Poseidon And you. A fine thing, I must say, a niece of mine, a senior goddess too, changing her mind.
Zeus Order, order!
Athene He's served his debt to society. Now he should go free.
Poseidon Go free. *He blinded my son the Cyclops*——
Athene To save his men!
Poseidon Insulted Tiresias in Hades! Ignored the Sirens, defied Scylla and Charybdis, ate the Sacred Cattle of the Sun-god——
Athene All to save his men!
Zeus And where are these men now, may I ask? Not also with Calypso, I hope. My word, these nymphs——
Athene Dead.
Zeus Dead?
Athene All dead.

Shocked silence

Drowned. Every one of them.
Poseidon And not before time. Serve them right. All liars!
Athene My lord, that remark is out of order!
Many Out of order! Out of order!
Zeus (*to Secretary*) Strike it from the record. Now look here, Poseidon, I've had just about enough——
Poseidon Enough! I've had enough!
Zeus You've had enough? You, my trumped-up little brother, I'll tell you when you've had enough. We'll vote on it, that's what we'll do, and then we'll see if you've had enough. (*To Athene*) Drowned, you say?
Athene Or slain when Poseidon threw his last thunderbolt. Since when Calypso has nursed him, fed him, clothed him——

Zeus Not if I know my little Calypso she hasn't——

Athene (*deciding to ignore this*) Until such time as this Council grants him permission to go home again.

Zeus And in this home in ... in——? (*He snaps his fingers*)

Secretary Ithaca.

Zeus There's a loving wife ...?

Secretary Penelope.

Athene And a loving son Telemachus, all but a babe when the mighty general sailed for Troy, but now a fine warrior, rising twenty, tall and strong——

Murmurs of appreciation from many of the company

Zeus (*hastily*) Enough, enough, behave yourselves!

Athene —who doesn't even know if his famous father still lives or not.

Zeus And this Penelope, does she know?

Athene No, great lord. In the meantime she is surrounded by a horde of zealous suitors who wish to marry her and claim all Ulysses' kingdom for themselves.

Zeus How does she keep them at bay?

All (*variations of*) Yes, how? I must say I don't blame them ... (*etc. etc.*)

Athene By spinning.

All Spinning?

Athene By spinning an endless garment, saying that when she has finished it, she'll decide whom to take as her new husband.

God It must be simply *endless* by now, Athene! How does she make it last?

Athene By unpicking at night what she has spun during the day.

Amazed silence from all. Until at last ...

God I say, what a spiffing idea.

Another Some gal.

Goddess A feminist after my own heart.

Huge appeciation. Some applause. Zeus tinkles his bell

Zeus Very well, lass, you've persuaded me. We'll have our vote and if all are agreed, I suggest you nip off to Ulysses and tell him to get home while the going's good. And while you're about it, look in at ... at——?

Secretary Ithaca.

Zeus —and have a word with that young Telemachus. Mind you, on second thoughts, I might do that myself.

Athene (*firmly*) I think I'd better, your lordship.

Zeus Ah, well. As for you, Poseidon, if the vote goes against you, let's have no more of your hanky-panky. If we say this Ulysses goes home, goes home he does. All agreed?

All Agreed!!

Poseidon Pah! Rigged! The whole damned Court's been rigged. I'll tell you this, brother. Whatever your little vote decides, Ulysses hasn't heard the end of this, not by a long chalk. Mark my words, I'm not finished yet! The man's a two-faced liar and criminal!

He storms out followed by his Attendants

Zeus Let's have the vote then. Then we can get off home. Yesses through that door. Noes through that one. Thanks for coming and being so good-natured about it.

The Court splits into two, making sure there are far more Yesses than Noes, and goes out the appropriate doors, chattering excitedly

(*Calling Athene*) Listen, daughter, I don't trust your uncle. He's a mean one in a scrape and he'll do for Ulysses as soon as look at him. So you get him home as soon as you can. There's a powerful lot of water to be crossed before he can get to Ithaca, remember.

Athene Thank you, Father.

They go out

Silence for a moment to allow the atmosphere to settle. The Lights go down to a pin-spot

Ulysses steps forward. Perhaps his beard is now grey. He speaks very simply

SCENE 2

Calypso's Island

Ulysses   I have been studying how I may compare
                    This island where I live unto the world:
                    And, for because the world is populous
                    And here is not a mortal but myself,
                    I cannot do it;—yet I'll hammer it out.
                    My brain I'll prove the female to my soul,
                    My soul the father: and these two beget
                    A generation of still-breeding thoughts.

So here goes. For seven years I've lived in this place with only Calypso the nymph for company. All else are dead, that whole happy band that sailed for Troy nearly twenty years ago, and still I'm mocked by the gods. Here's no ship, no means at all to venture to Poseidon's sea. One step in that direction and I'd be sunk without compunction. So what am I to do? You may ask, why don't you defy the god? But what form would that take, and in any case, I've done it before and look where it got me. No, I now believe the gods are probably there to be obeyed. All nature seems to conform to a strict pattern from the heavens to the earth, and we defy this organized system of degree at our very peril.

During the following Calypso and Athene enter together and stay watching quietly as Ulysses speaks

                    The heavens themselves, the planets and this centre,
                    Observe degree, priority and place,
                    Insisture, course, proportion, season, form,

Office and custom, in all line of order.
But when degree is shaked,
Which is the ladder to all high designs,
The enterprise is sick. What plagues, what portents.
What mutiny! What raging of the sea! Shaking of earth!
Take but degree away and see what discord follows—
Commotion in the winds! Frights, changes, horrors,
Divert and crack, rend and deracinate
The unity and married calm of states
Quite apart from their fixture.

No, no, this I now believe, this order must be maintained to keep the universal spinning. The gods must be obeyed from first to last and in defying them I have received my just deserts. So sit on, Ulysses, this is the conclusion I reach every day, your punishment must continue, to be mocked by the gods and forgotten by men for the rest of time.

Calypso (*to Athene*) In answer to your question, great goddess, no, he hasn't always been like this. For the first five years he was full of hope, of plans to build a ship and sail alone to Ithaca. But recently his resolution's drained away. He sees himself living here forever. My love gives him strength to go from day to day, but after that—in the matter of years— I'm powerless to help him.

Athene That's where I come in. I may have a plan to help him. Leave us for a while. Let me speak to him.

Calypso I beg you do, great Athene. My love's so strong I'd sooner see him go and live, than stay and die.

Calypso leaves

Athene Now, mighty Zeus, lend me your tongue to persuade him. (*She moves forward*) Great general, mighty Ulysses, grant me your attention for a moment.

A long pause. He turns and looks at her

We've met before.
Ulysses I know the face but not the name.
Athene Before the walls of Troy.
Ulysses So long ago?
Athene You knew me then.

He nods. It's as if he'd been expecting her

Ulysses Athene, great goddess. I knew it. You've come to prolong my punishment. Well, speak. From ten years, make it twenty. Why not thirty?
Athene Not at all. I've come to end it.
Ulysses Mockery still? End it?
Athene You're free to go.
Ulysses Free? And Zeus agrees?
Athene We all agree. Except ...
Ulysses (*bitterly*) Except Poseidon? And there's the rub. There is no other

way to leave this place except by Poseidon's sea. I'll get a mile offshore and then he'll drown me like the others.

Athene Not at all. Come, Ulysses, use your nimble wits. You've been given permission to return to Ithaca. Seize the moment. Your wife awaits. So does your son.

Ulysses (*brightening for a moment*) They're alive?

Athene And still thinking of you, but not for much longer if you don't get a move on.

Ulysses What's the use? I tell you, nothing will change Poseidon's mind.

Athene (*irritated*) For the gods' sake, stop whining. Where's the mighty Ulysses we used to know?

Ulysses Gone. Quite gone. Gone with the rest of his comrades that he led to their death.

Athene What nonsense! You're alive. More alive than ever. Even a little plump. Sleek almost. And you're rested. Calypso has done a good job. Seven years of home cooking and the creature comforts. The trouble is ... you've been spoiled.

Ulysses (*gloomily*) She'll never let me go.

Athene You're wrong. She'll be pleased to see the end of you. When you arrived you were the mighty general the whole world had heard about— strong, resolute, full of courage. Now you're just a shadow of that man, neutered and fat.

Ulysses (*stung*) Not at all! That man still! Ha!

Athene Then prove it! Leave now! Challenge Poseidon. Use your royal blood to show you have not changed.

Ulysses How? The Sea-God will not rest? Wherever I go he'll see me. And there is no ship, no way to reach Ithaca. Do you expect me to *walk*?

Athene (*laughing*) That's more like the hero I used to know. No, I don't expect you to walk. You'll ... drift.

Ulysses Drift?

Athene I won't explain. We've spent too long talking as it is. Come, his spies are assembling already.

The Lights darken slightly. The squawking of sea birds is heard distantly

(*Calling*) Calypso! Quick, say your farewells.

Calypso appears

She and Ulysses stand facing each other. They raise their hands so their palms brush

Ulysses For all your love, I thank you.

Calypso Go well. May the gods lead you to your happiness.

Ulysses So much pain still to be endured.

Calypso The memory of our love will sustain you.

The sound of the sea birds increases. One or two of the cast race across the stage or hover, looking down

Athene Enough. The spies are almost here. Come, we need driftwood.

They leave hastily

More Seagulls sweep in. Some circle, others squat on high places. The movement of their wings is slow and controlled, but their head gestures are sharp and predatory

Seagull 1 We are there, Poseidon. We have reached Calypso's island.
Seagull 2 And stretch from here to Ithaca.
Seagull 3 Dozens of us.
Seagull 4 Hundreds.
Seagull 5 More than you can count.
Poseidon (*on amplifier*) Go to it, my beauties, my little hounds of heaven. Keep your eyes glued to every living thing on that sea of mine.
Seagull 1 We obey.
Seagull 2 Nothing will escape our gaze.
Seagull 3 The eyesight of a bird is known to be sharper than the sharpest knife.
Seagull 4 Nothing can escape the eye of a flying creature that wants to see.
Seagull 5 And of all flying creatures, that of a seagull is the clearest of all.
Seagull 1 Look!
Seagull 2 Where?
Seagull 3 To the east.
Seagull 4 A ship!
Seagull 5 A trading vessel. I'll investigate. (*He moves off*)
Seagull 1 And in the west another.
Seagull 2 A fishing boat.
Seagull 3 No Ulysses.
Seagull 1 Check! Check! Poseidon will never forgive us if we let him escape.

General movement. They add their own sounds to those from off stage

Seagull 5 No Ulysses. No Ulysses.
Seagull 1 No Ulysses.
Seagull 2 Keep looking.
Seagull 3 There!
Seagull 4 Where?
Seagull 5 Down below.
Seagull 1 Driftwood.
Seagull 2 Can we be sure?
Seagull 3 Only driftwood.

Athene appears for a moment

Athene Good speed, Ulysses. May Zeus lead you safely home. Now I'll to Ithaca before you and speak to Telemachus. He must prepare for your return.

She leaves

Seagull 4 I don't like the look of that driftwood.
Seagull 5 It's not big enough for a raft.
Seagull 1 And there's no man on it.

Seagull 2 What if he's beneath it?
Seagull 3 No man could be so clever.
Seagull 4 And how would he breathe?
Seagull 5 Exactly. Look, another ship!
Seagull 1 Where?
Seagull 2 To the north!
Seagull 3 Let's investigate that. It looks more hopeful.

They all rise. The noise increases to very loud shrill shrieking and then they all sweep out

The Lights go down. Silence. Ulysses speaks unseen

Ulysses (*off*) I only hope I can make it. Breathing through a straw is very difficult.

SCENE 3

Ithaca

Fast music sweeps in from off stage. This is the only section in which something like Rock or Heavy Metal can be used, but nothing familiar. A door opens in the dark, spilling light and louder music into the acting area. A pause. Then it slams shut, closing off light and sound again. Telemachus speaks in the dark

Telemachus Mother?

The Light comes up on Penelope at her spinning wheel

Penelope I'm here, Telemachus.
Telemachus They're calling for you again.
Penelope Let them wait.
Telemachus They won't for much longer. They're determined to end this farce. Antinous in particular. He swears he'll marry you before the week is out.
Penelope He may, he may.
Telemachus Then why not give in gracefully? Accept him now and stop this dreaming. He'd make a good husband, when all's said and done.
Penelope And a good father, Telemachus? Is that it? Have you stopped believing in your father's return?
Telemachus Twenty years is a long time to remember somebody who never really existed in the first place. When I was a child it was easy to believe in him. Just to touch his second-best suit of armour, to handle the Great Bow that hangs in the Banquet Hall, all these were enough to remind me of that big booming voice.
Penelope You were such a loving child.
Telemachus Then when I grew older ... seven ... eight ... just the stories of his bravery in the war were enough to kindle my faith. The tales coming out of Troy always spoke of his iron will, his strength and his wizardry in battle.

Penelope Even as a boy you always loved heroes. And of them all, your father was surely the greatest you could think of.

Telemachus But it was when we'd heard Troy had fallen that my love was at its fiercest. To see him again, to feel the warmth of his blood that could easily scald somebody standing too close——

Penelope (*a kind smile*) He was only a man, Telemachus, not a god.

Telemachus No! To me he was always a god!

Penelope (*gently*) And has this god died then that you no longer believe?

Telemachus I don't know. I only know the time has come to stop dreaming. If he comes, he comes. If not, not. In the meantime Antinuous would make a good husband.

Penelope We'll see, we'll see. When I've finished this spinning.

Telemachus (*turning away*) That's all you ever say.

Athene speaks from the shadows

Athene Telemachus?

Telemachus Who speaks?

Athene Here. In the dark. Come close.

Telemachus Who are you? I cannot see you.

She moves forward slightly so that we recognize her. She wears a veil over her head

Athene That's of no importance. But tell me first, what's that noise coming from the Palace?

Telemachus (*a shrug*) My mother's suitors. Ever since my father's disappearance, our house has been infested with these enemies. Day and night the revels continue as they ply the Queen with proposals of marriage. Great feasting and ribaldry are the order of the day. Our life as rulers is in ruins. Soon they'll have eaten us out of house and home. Our estates will be overrun and our reign at an end.

Athene What will your mother do?

Telemachus In sheer self-defence she'll have to marry one of them in the end, else all will be lost. I'd hoped my father's return would put a stop to it all, but after nineteen years I must admit I'm giving up hope.

Athene Then know, Telemachus, son of the mighty Ulysses, I have some news for you.

Telemachus (*mocking*) Ulysses is coming home, I suppose.

Athene I didn't say that. But a stranger has arrived on your shore, a poor man, destitute, worn out. Make your secret way to the beach. You'll find him there. Go now, but remember, tell no-one, not even your mother—specially your mother—of this man. But believe, believe all he tells you.

The door opens from the Palace spilling light and music over the acting area. Two Suitors enter. The door closes again

Go now. And may the gods spare you.

She disappears into the shadows

The Suitors pass nearby. They are not completely sober, but not "falling down

*drunk". They carry a bottle which they share and head for Penelope's lighted
area. Telemachus waits until they're out of ear-shot and then calls softly*

Telemachus Great goddess—for that is whom I believe you to be—listen to
this prayer.

The figure in white reappears. In fact it's a double

For nearly twenty years I've waited for this moment and something tells
me it's nearly over. If it's true this stranger has news of my father's return,
I, Telemachus swear to the gods, I shall repay his arrival with much piety
and devotion. May the gods seal our pact with my blood if I fail to
do so.

Suitors Penelope .. ooh, Penelope? When will your spinning be finished?

Penelope (*unpicking the work she has done*) Soon ... soon ...

Suitors (*arguing*) It's me she'll marry. No, me!

Suitor 1 If it's you, promise me I'll get half of whatever she has.

Suitor 2 Done! And if she marries you, I'll have Mondays, Wednesday and
Fridays! And all the public holidays.

Suitor 1 'S a bargain. Anybody but that boring Antinuououous!

Suitor 2 'S fact. Come, lesh go back to the party ...

They weave their way out into the dark

The Light fades on Penelope

Telemachus Is it a bargain?

The figure nods and extends a hand. He kneels and kisses it

*She goes out and immediately the "real" Athene enters from another part
to join Ulysses who is lying sprawled out on the floor. She wakes him*

Athene Ulysses, wake. You are home.

Ulysses (*stirring*) I dreamt you were talking to my son at the Palace.

Athene A goddess can be in two places at once, can't she? Now listen well.
Even though you're back in Ithaca your troubles aren't over. You are
surrounded by enemies quite prepared to kill you if they find out who
you are. You must keep your wits about you.

A great shrieking and calling as the seagulls appear

Seagull 1 It's Ulysses! It's Ulysses! We've found him!

Seagulls Found him! Found him! Found him!

*They surround Ulysses and Athene aggressively, making pecking and clawing
movements*

Athene Back, harpies! This is no place for you. Poseidon's kingdom ends
at the water's edge. All this land and the earth beyond belong to my
father, the great Thunderer Zeus. Don't offend him, I warn you. Ulysses
is home now and a king in his kingdom. You cannot touch him now.

The Birds withdraw reluctantly, hissing balefully. As Telemachus approaches, they fly up, calling furiously

Seagulls Too late, too late! Poseidon will never forgive us! We have failed, failed, failed ...

The mournful cry of seagulls takes over as they move out, and then fades away

Athene Here comes your son now. Remember what I told you and do exactly as I commanded.

She watches for a moment and then leaves quietly

Telemachus (*approaching warily*) Sir, I was told you have news for me.

Ulysses If you are the one I seek.

Telemachus Sir, I am Telemachus, prince of this kingdom, only son of the hero Ulysses, great commander of this place.

Ulysses Ulysses, eh? I've heard of him. Tell me, lordly prince, is your father here?

Telemachus No, good sir, I wish he were, but he's still not returned from the war at Troy.

Ulysses The war at Troy? My, my, that was a long time ago.

Telemachus Ten years, sir, all but a few months. Tell me, sir, were you not there, for something in the way you spoke the name tells me you were?

Ulysses Ay, that I was and saw your father there many times. Why, when he led the attack on the temple I was right beside him. (*Hastily*) But I shouldn't boast of that. Athene was mightily offended by his action, I promise you.

Telemachus And after Troy you saw him not at all?

Ulysses Oh, here and there, here and there.

Telemachus Then do you think he lives?

Ulysses Do you?

Telemachus At this moment, sir, I do.

Ulysses Then he does, for nobody ever really dies as long as we think of them with love. He had a dog once, I seem to remember ...

Telemachus Argus! He still lives, but fitfully now, so old he barely has the strength to wag his tail. But say "Ulysses" to him and he'll prick his ears and lick your hand in such a way it would bring tears to your eyes.

Ulysses In truth it does to mine simply to hear of it. And his old nurse Eurycleia, does she still breathe?

Telemachus As lustily as I do myself. Oh, many's the time she's told me of my father as a child. The day he tripped over the milking stool and scarred his knee.

Ulysses I have such a scar, but I fear me I cannot see it, for my eyes are too full of tears.

Telemachus And mine too, but I saw it before I started to weep. Oh, my Father, you are welcome.

Ulysses And you are blessed for saying it .. oh, I've learnt so much!

They embrace. The Lights go down on them

Ulysses I and II step forward

Ulysses I So he came home. After ten long years of wandering——
Ulysses II —and the many extraordinary adventures you have seen and
many others we didn't have time to show you.
Ulysses I But the dangers weren't over yet.
Ulysses II For if the Suitors knew he had returned——
Ulysses I —they would certainly kill him.
Ulysses II While to reclaim his kingdom and his Queen, he would certainly
have to kill them.
Ulysses I So to the last adventure——
Ulysses II —the Defeat of the Suitors!

SCENE 4

The Reunion

The fast music explodes in our ears as the stage blazes with light

*The rest of the cast stream on and within a moment we are in the midst of a
noisy, colourful feast. Besides the Suitors in their splendid robes and flowing
whiskers, there are their beautiful wives and girl-friends, courtiers of all
kinds, servants, bodyguards, palace officials and pages. For the moment only
Penelope, Telemachus and Ulysses are missing, but everybody else who can
be found, should be there*

Suitor (*above the uproar*) Tell us about the boar-hunt, Antinuous! Was it
good sport?
Others The boar-hunt! The boar-hunt!
Antinuous Ye gods, the damned thing was twice as big as a house!
Others (*laughing*) As a house? Antinuous is bragging again!
Antinuous I tell you, he came out of the forest like an arrow out of a bow,
tusks at the ready, just scraping the ground. I took up my spear——
All He took up his spear!
Antinuous My horse reared——
All His horse reared!
Antinuous It nearly threw me——
Suitor It did, it did. I saw it. Antinuous hung on for dear life——
Lady (*to a friend*) I must say if we go on like this I'm going to demand
boredom money from Penelope. The thought of having to listen to
Antinuous at any more of these boring parties——
Friend But beautiful, my dear. Now if it were fat old Kristos telling the
stories——
Lady Fat old Kristos on a boar-hunt . . .?
Others What are you two laughing at?
Others Quiet there! Antinuous is telling us about the greatest boar-hunt in
history!

General laughter

Lady The greatest bore hunting the greatest boar!

More laughter

Antinuous I tell you he was the swarthiest, the hairiest, the most ravening beast in all creation.

Delighted cries of appreciation

Suitor It was, it was, I saw it!

Antinuous And to make matters worse I'd already used my longest spear on the first brute. Now getting down on one knee, I aimed my stabbing lance at his jugular. On he came like some damned machine, all sweating and straining——

Telemachus enters during the next

Lady Just like the hunter!

Laughter

Antinuous And *drove* itself on to the blade so that blood and gore shot everywhere——

Lady Oh, how *disgusting*——

Another My dear, it's an animal. You can't expect it to have good manners . . .

The story continues, but more quietly now and improvised to suit the players

Eumaeus, an old servant, approaches Telemachus

Eumaeus The stranger has arrived, young master, and asks permission to pass among your guests.

Telemachus Make him welcome, Eumaeus. And if any should challenge him, have him take the matter up with me.

Eumaeus goes off and presently we see him leading Ulysses to a stool in the corner. The latter is now putting on an act as a very old beggar-man, all bent and trembling and dressed in rags

Guests passing with food and drink look at him askance sitting in the corner

Eurycleia, has my mother come down yet?

Eurycleia Not yet, young master. She asked to be called when the contest with the Long Bow starts. (*She is Ulysses' old nurse, a strong forthright old body of uncertain years*)

Telemachus I'll see to it. In the meantime that old beggar there needs refreshment. Look to it, will you?

Eurycleia Willingly, young master. (*Approaching Ulysses*) How now, old sir, have you brought your stomach with you?

Ulysses Enough to consume this lot, that's for sure.

Eurycleia God save you, we've better fare for your digestion than this. Now there's pasties and pies and honey cakes with cloves—— (*She breaks off and looks at him more closely*) How now, have we met before, old man? There's something familiar about your smell.

Ulysses (*offended*) My smell? What do you mean?

Eurycleia The way your skin smells ... now I haven't smelled that particular aroma for ... oh, I don't know how many years. And your hands ... there's something familiar about your nails, chewed and bitten as they are. Do I know you?

Ulysses (*very calm*) Not unless you don't value your life, Eurycleia. Now listen very quietly. Many's the time you've cut these selfsame nails in a bowl of water to stop me writhing with pretended torment, and commented too on the particular smell of my hair after a bath ...

Eurycleia Oh, Zeus ... is it you?

Ulysses Be still, old heart, and don't give the game away. I knew I could not keep the news from you, but apart from you only Telemachus knows. Not even my wife. And if this lot found out ...

Eurycleia They'd kill you and that's for sure.

Ulysses So keep your palpitations to yourself and fetch me some of those honey cakes you spoiled me with as a child.

Eurycleia (*as she goes*) The gods be blessed. The dearest miracle has come to pass ...

The Chamberlain knocks with his staff for silence

Chamberlain Silence for the Prince Telemachus.

Some mockery which soon settles into an expectant silence

Telemachus My lord Suitors, your long patience is about to be rewarded. This very night my mother will announce whom she is to marry.

Amazement and excitement. A buzz of conversation

Antinuous What's happened to the "endless garment", Telemachus? Has it been completed at last?

Laughter

Telemachus On my suggestion it's been set aside. Instead there is to be the Contest of the Long Bow.

He nods to Eumaeus who comes forward with an elaborately decorated long bow of intimidating size. Telemachus holds it up for all to see

Many of you will recognize my father's special bow. Ever since his departure for Troy it has hung over his throne in the banquet hall. Now, whoever can draw this bow and send an arrow through a line of rings diminishing in size to strike a target will have a claim on the Queen's hand.

Enormous excitement. Applause and chatter. Many of the Suitors shout their right to try it

Suitor 1 I shall do it! I have the straightest eye in all Ithaca!

Suitor 2 Ay, when it squints sideways.

Laughter

But I have the straightest looking forward!

Suitor 3 It's not a straight eye you need, but a straight arrow.

Suitor 4 And a steady hand. Everybody knows I have the steadiest grip in all Greece.

Suitor 5 For drinking, but not for aiming.

More laughter

Let me try. I'll show you how to do it. A steady arm comes from steady legs. See? (*He demonstrates to his friends*)

Meanwhile . . .

Antinuous How will your mother choose, Telemachus, for at least a dozen of us will put the test to shame?

All Ay, ay! How will she choose the winner?

Telemachus That will depend on the number. You see here the famous Long Bow. In his time only the mighty Ulysses had the strength to draw it. Now let us see who has the strongest arm as well as the straightest eye.

Suitor 6 Pooh! That's no test at all. Ulysses wasn't that strong. Besides we were all children when he was a young man. No wonder we couldn't do it then.

Suitor 7 Exactly! Now we're all grown men and quite used to drawing on the tightest bow.

Telemachus Then let's see who'll win the Contest and the Queen!

A roar of applause. The Chamberlain bangs with his staff

Chamberlain Queen Penelope approaches!

Everybody bows

Penelope enters with her Attendants

Telemachus goes forward to greet her

Penelope (*quietly*) Are you sure this is such a good idea, Telemachus? What if nobody wins?

Telemachus Then you'll marry nobody, Mother.

Penelope And if the wrong man wins?

Telemachus Only the right man can win it, Mother. That is the purpose of the Contest. (*To the Suitors*) Now prepare! Here are the rings!

The Suitors jostle to draw lots to see who will go first. While they are doing this, the rest of the Court form themselves into two facing lines holding aloft metal rings of diminishing size. The last can be off stage so the target is not seen. Or the rings can be mimed by holding up curled fingers. The drumbeats start

Come, who is to start?

Tessipus It is I, Tessipus!

Telemachus Excellent, Tessipus. I think you would make a good father, but an elderly husband.

Laughter

Give him the bow, Eumaeus.

The bow is presented. Silence falls. Tessipus mimes fitting an arrow and raises the bow to aim down the line of rings. But when he comes to draw the string, he cannot do it

Antinuous Come, Tessipus, you're too feeble. Let us younger ones have a go.

Tessipus No, no, I love Penelope as much as you. I swear I have the strength. (*He tries again. And fails again*)

Ridicule and merriment. Tessipus is jostled out of the way

Telemachus Who have we now? Agelaus? Come, you can do it, I'm sure.

Agelaus tries and also fails. So does Clymenus. And Eurymachus

Antinuous Come, this is ridiculous. Who strung the bow, Telemachus? He who strung it would surely have the strength to draw it.

Telemachus My father strung it before he went to Troy. Since then none has had the strength to loosen it, so its remained like this ever since.

Antinuous Except me. I'll show you how it's done.

Others Wait your turn, wait your turn! Then you can show us.

Antinuous I don't mind going last. It will give you all a chance to fail.

Jeers and ridicule

Some Can you do it, Telemachus? If so, show us.

Telemachus I don't have to. Penelope is my mother. I don't wish to marry her.

Others Then let Antinuous try.

The cry is taken up

All Antinuous ... Antinuous .. Antinuous ...!

Antinuous If you insist. (*He takes the bow*) So, Telemachus, prepare to greet your new father. And remember, if your first one should return, it will be the grave for him. I'll brook no rivals in your mother's bed.

Excitement. Cheers. While Antinuous prepares his stance and receives advice from his cronies, Ulysses calls Telemachus to his side

Ulysses The moment is approaching. It's exactly as I planned. Have your men move round the hall and collect up all the weapons the Suitors have left there. Then await the signal I alone shall give.

Telemachus nods and takes Eumaeus and the Chamberlain aside. They go quietly about their task, collecting whatever swords and spears the Suitors have laid aside. Meanwhile Antinuous takes his stance, feet planted firmly apart, inserts the arrow and bringing the bow slowly to eye-level, attempts to haul back on the string. And cannot do it. Consternation

Some Look! Even he can't do it!

Others Try again, Antinuous. No bow can beat you.
Antinuous (*with a laugh*) That was just a siting stance. Now I'll pierce the
    target and the lady's heart at one!

*The drum beats faster. Antinuous repeats the preparation and struggles ...
and struggles to draw the string. And fails once more. Uproar*

All (*variations of*) Even Antinuous cannot do it? Now what will happen?
    Who will marry the Queen now? Is it a plot? What is Telemachus planning?

The drum ends on a crash. Ulysses stands, still a frail old man

Ulysses There is still one more to try.

They all turn and look at him. Silence. Then huge merriment

All (*variations of*) You, old man? Tessipus was old enough, but you could
    be *his* father! What's this, Penelope, will you marry grave-birds? As it is
    he hasn't the strength to move let alone anything else!
Telemachus Give him the bow. Let him try.
Antinuous (*furious*) Never! Would you insult us by letting beggars compete?
Others Ay, that's an insult! Damned impertinence!
Some Not at all! Let him try! Why should the contest not be open to all?
Penelope Telemachus, are you sure you know what you're doing? I don't
    know if I want to marry this old man. He looks near death to me.
Telemachus Trust me, Mother. He's the nearest thing to life in this whole
    Palace. (*Calling*) The Queen commands. Let the stranger have the bow.

*Antinuous hesitates. He is still holding the bow. He is still furious at the insult.
He gives way with very bad grace*

Antinuous Very well, madam, if that's the way your taste runs, I'll have no
    more part of this.

Eurycleia takes the bow from him and brings it to Ulysses

Eurycleia (*quietly*) Now, master, take the bow and my lady's heart and all
    this mighty kingdom into your hand once more.

*Ulysses nods and walks slowly to his place. Silence except for a steady
thumping off stage*

Telemachus What's that noise, Eurycleia?

She takes a quick look

Eurycleia Why, it's Argus, young master, thumping his tail. I believe he's
    recognized his lord already.
Telemachus May the gods bless him, so have we all.

*Ulysses takes up his position with the bow. With great deliberation he mimes
placing the arrow, then stance well held, weight on the forward foot, he brings
the arrow to eye-level, at the same time transferring his weight to the back
foot. A pause. The watchers hold their breath. Then he draws back the string
as far as his chin. A gasp of astonishment. And releases the imaginary arrow.*

Those holding the rings follow its progress with a swift turning of their heads—WHOOSH! There is a clang from off stage and a cry of amazement

All He's done it! The old man's done it!

Perhaps the barking of Argus is added to the tumult. But Ulysses wastes no time. Throwing off his act as the old man, he stands upright and bellows

Ulysses Now, Telemachus, the time is here! I am Ulysses, returned from the dead, lord of this lady and all these lands! Strike all traitors down for I am here to reclaim my own!

Wholesale panic ensues. Legend tells us that he and his followers cut down all the traitors who had come to live at his Court. Drumbeats and music accompany the action which should be as stylized as possible. Whichever way it is done, either as a slow-motion dance like the advance on Troy in the first scene, or as confused, running action, the sequence should last at least two minutes to carry its full dramatic weight

Telemachus Bar the doors, Eumaeus! Let no-one out!
Eumaeus It is done, master!
Telemachus And post men outside and guard the gates. Let no-one in!
Eumaeus That too is done!

All being shouted above the uproar

Antinuous God in heaven, where is my sword? I left it here!
Another And my hunting spears! I am unarmed!
Another So are we all! Ulysses, is this what you consider fair battle?
Ulysses Traitors all! You have plotted my death many times. Now plot your own!
Ulysses I (*in another part*) I AM ULYSSES OF THE NIMBLE WITS. My vengeance is terrible and my revenge is sweet!
Ulysses II (*in yet another part of the acting area*) I AM ULYSSES, SON OF ROYAL LAERTES. I seek only what is mine, my wife, my son and my kingdom!
Antinuous Ye gods, how many of him are there?
Another He's everywhere at once!
Ulysses Slay them all, Telemachus! None must escape!
Telemachus There is Tessipus, Father. He was a loyal man.
Ulysses Slay them all I say! The god will know who is innocent.
Telemachus No, Father. Zeus would not approve butchery.
Suitor Heaven spare us, they are killing the women as well!
Ulysses I Are they any less guilty than their men? Did they not plot as well?
Ulysses II Would they not surplant Penelope and rule the land in her place?
Eurycleia (*to Penelope*) Come, madam, this slaughterhouse is no place for you.
Penelope No, Eurycleia, my place is in my Palace and at my husband's side.
Chamberlain There is fighting in the town. The army has risen in support of Ulysses!
Telemachus Father, strike to your left! There are assassins there!

Ulysses I And here!
Ulysses II And here!

Ulysses stands on a box. A rope hangs conveniently close. He seizes it and swings across the action to another part of the acting area. Thunder cracks. The drum crashes. The Lights go down to strobe. The sound of trumpets off and a great mass of people shouting and fighting. Floodlights normally standing in the wings, now appear and are trundled forward, closing on the actors, the great lights blazing like headlamps. More music. More thunder

Ulysses I am Ulysses, the ever-crafty, conqueror of Troy, general and sailor, scourge of the mighty Cyclops, lover of Circe and the beautiful Calypso and I'll tell you this. I AM HOME AGAIN and RIGHTFUL OWNER OF ALL THESE LANDS.
Antinuous Spare us, Ulysses!
Ulysses I Never!
Ulysses II Never!
Ulysses Never!
Antinous There must be more of them than stars in heaven!
All Ulysses (*stabbing him*) We are everywhere!
Antinuous Gods, I die!
All Ulysses In your time, Antinuous, and that is *now*!

The carnage draws to a close. The strobe ends and the Lights return to normal. The floodlights retreat. The drumbeats fade away and so does the distant sound of fighting in the town

Telemachus Now the battle has been won and retribution done. Madam, do you accept the right man won the Contest?
Penelope I accept. (*To Ulysses*) Sir, will you live with me and be my husband after all these many years?
Ulysses That I will, if it please the gods.

Athene appears

Athene It pleases them, Ulysses.
Poseidon (*on amplifier*) All except me.
Athene Then remember what Tiresias said. To placate my uncle, take up an oar and tramp to the furthest part of your kingdom and even beyond, to a place where people will not know what it is you carry. There bury it and make sacrifices to Poseidon. Only then may you live in peace with your wife and son.
Ulysses I (*to the audience*) So off we set again.
Ulysses II Huffing and puffing, carrying an oar——
Ulysses I —looking something of an idiot, I can tell you.
Ulysses II But what the god wills must be obeyed. At least I'd learned that.

An oar is produced by Eumaeus and passed to Telemachus who hands it to the three Ulysses. They shoulder it and set off in line round and round the acting area. The "dead" resurrect themselves and stand all about the stage so that the trio is forced to weave its way around them

Telemachus (*to the audience*) It took a long time, I can tell you, trying to find somebody who couldn't recognize an oar.

Eumaeus Years and years in fact. Nor was there any shortage of cheeky ones?

Child 'Ere, mister, where you going wiv that oar?

Old woman No use bringing that here. There ain't no water here, you know.

Man Looking for a boat, are you?

Telemachus Years and years . . .

Three bowler hats are brought in and handed to the Ulysses, followed by a brief-case, an umbrella, and a copy of "The Times". Still they walk

Eumaeus On and on they went . . .

Chamberlain From one century to the next . . .

Penelope Right up to the present day!

Athene Until finally——

Old man Goodness gracious me, what have you got there? Is it . . . is it really a cricket bat?

Ulysses I A cricket bat?

Ulysses II A cricket bat?

Ulysses III A cricket bat?

They consult. All nod

All Ulysses YES, A CRICKET BAT!

Telemachus So finally they had won! They'd found somebody who didn't know what an oar was.

Old man (*to the audience*) Actually I did know, but I think a little lie sometimes helps things along.

Ulysses I So the oar was buried deep.

Ulysses II And sacrifices made to Poseidon.

Ulysses III Lord Poseidon, please forgive us.

Poseidon (*on amplifier*) Well, if I have to . . .

All Ulysses Please!

Poseidon (*on amplifier*) Well . . . all right.

The final music starts, a triumph and a celebration

Ulysses I So now we set off home.

Ulysses II Where you'll be going shortly.

Ulysses III To rejoin Penelope and Telemachus and live happily ever after.

Telemachus Except it wasn't quite like that. He soon talked himself into trouble again.

All Ulysses, look! An eagle!

Zeus is revealed on a rock, holding out his arms like wings

Ulysses Mighty Zeus! (*He kneels*) Thank you for appearing. I don't want you to think I'm ungrateful, but . . .

Zeus What is it now, Ulysses?

Ulysses Much as I love Penelope . . . is there any chance of going back to Calypso? She really was very beautiful.

Zeus reacts with horror. So does everybody else

Zeus ULYSSES? AFTER ALL THIS?

Ulysses Oh, dear, I'm sorry, lord Zeus. (*To the audience*) I dare say I'd
better settle for what I've got. Actually it's what I planned in the first
place, you know.

Penelope and Telemachus move forward to greet him

Penelope Welcome home, dear husband.

Ulysses Thank you, my dear. Oh, well, here I am at last.

Telemachus Welcome home, Father. (*He gives the first shout*) Ulysses!
Mighty warrior! Home at last!

All Ulysses! Ulysses! Ulysses! Ulysses! Home at last!

Athene Consider this. The greatest revelation is in stillness. Therefore, be
still . . .

The cast count 5 silently. The mirror-ball revolves

All (*a long drawn-out breath*) Ulysses . . .

They remain absolutely still. After a while the Lights go down

BLACK-OUT

FURNITURE AND PROPERTY LIST

ACT I

On stage: Rostrum
Dolphin throne on high rostrum

Off stage: Kit (**Soldiers**)
Bowls of fruit (**Lotus-Eaters**)
Map (**Bosun**)
Dummy Sailors (**Stage Management**)
Staff (optional) (**Ulysses**)
Large leather bag (**Sons** and **Daughters**)
Carpet, cushions, bowls of fruit and wine (**Girls**)
Beeswax, rope (**Sailors**)

Personal: **Ulysses**: curly beard, sword (required throughout)
Poseidon: trident
Soldiers: swords, spears, shields
Attackers: weird masks
Refugees: bundles
Peasant: staff, herb

ACT II

On stage: Benches
Table. *On it*: carafe of water, tumbler, notebooks, small handbell

Off stage: Brief-cases, files, documents (**Gods** and **Goddesses**)
Pile of files (**Secretary**)
Spinning wheel (**Penelope**)
Bottle (**Suitors**)
Food and drink (**Cast**)
Stool (**Stage Management**)
Long bow (**Eumaeus**)
Metal rings (**Court**)
Box, rope hanging down (**Stage Management**)
Floodlights (**Stage Management**)
Oar (**Eumaeus**)
3 bowler hats, brief-case, umbrella, copy of *The Times* (**Stage Management**)

Personal: **Poseidon**: trident
Chamberlain: staff
Suitors: swords, spears

LIGHTING PLOT

Practical fittings required: mirror-ball, strobe, floodlights

An open stage

ACT I

To open: Black-out

Cue 1   When ready   (Page 1)
Light on mirror-ball as it spins, faster and faster

Cue 2   **Poseidon**: "... hear this my curse."   (Page 1)
Slowly bring up light on **Poseidon**, *high on his throne*

Cue 3   As sound of city at war arises   (Page 2)
Fade light on **Poseidon**; *searchlights sweep floor in all directions; fade light on mirror-ball; red glow of smoke and flame behind cut-out of walls and towers of Troy*

Cue 4   **Soldiers** wait in the shadows   (Page 2)
Searchlights grow more desperate

Cue 5   As **Soldiers** advance   (Page 2)
Searchlights move frantically, sometimes fading to near darkness, then coming up through sickly greens to midnight blues

Cue 6   **Refugees** lament   (Page 3)
Flashes of lightning; in distance, Troy flames and then slowly darkens

Cue 7   **Ulysses** is left alone   (Page 6)
Fade down to spot on **Ulysses**

Cue 8   **Ulysses**: "... we're only human."   (Page 7)
Increase lighting

Cue 9   **Zeus**: "... you've gone too far."   (Page 7)
Light on **Athene**, *high up*

Cue 10   **Athene**: "... won't last forever."   (Page 9)
Fade light on **Athene**

Cue 11   **Sailors** start to row strongly   (Page 9)
Golden lighting on boat

Cue 12   As rest of cast attack   (Page 11)
Fade lights to almost nothing

Cue 13   Attackers exit   (Page 11)
Increase lighting

Cue 14   **Ulysses II**: "We'll sail at dawn."   (Page 12)
             Fade down to night, then slowly fade up to dawn

Cue 15   **Sailor 4**: "... the stars beneath us."   (Page 12)
             Fade to deep night; light on mirror-ball as it spins

Cue 16   As SCENE 3 begins   (Page 13)
             Fade star effect; keep low lighting

Cue 17   As **Cyclops** mimes rolling huge stone   (Page 17)
             Fade lighting slightly on coral

Cue 18   **Ulysses**: "... until we'd solved that."   (Page 19)
             Narrow lighting down to **Sailors**, *with pin-spot on Cyclops*

Cue 19   **Cyclops** mimes rolling big rock away   (Page 21)
             Increase lighting

Cue 20   Waves lie down to rest   (Page 22)
             Fade to night

Cue 21   As SCENE 5 begins   (Page 22)
             Increase lighting

Cue 22   **Crew** settle down once more   (Page 23)
             Fade to night

Cue 23   **Helmsman**: "... for love or witchcraft ...."   (Page 23)
             Light on **Circe**

Cue 24   **Circe**: "Hear me and obey."   (Page 24)
             Cut light on **Circe**

Cue 25   **Ulysses**: "... and stay on watch."   (Page 24)
             Light on **Circe**

Cue 26   **Circe**: "... Ulysses, and obey."   (Page 24)
             Cut light on **Circe**

Cue 27   **Men** start off   (Page 25)
             Light on **Circe**

Cue 28   **Circe**: "... mark my voice and obey."   (Page 25)
             Cut light on **Circe**

Cue 29   **Helmsman**: "Ay, ay, sir."   (Page 25)
             Fade lights on ship; concentrate on **Sailors**

Cue 30   **Circe** makes a gesture   (Page 27)
             Change to warm, interior lighting

Cue 31   **Pigs** stand and raise a cheer of relief   (Page 28)
             Fade lights on feast; lights on **Sailors** *as they move forward*

Cue 32   **Ulysses**: "... a damnable place."   (Page 29)
             Quickly fade down to small spot on **Ulysses**

Cue 33   **Ulysses**: "... special to everyone."   (Page 29)
             Fade spot on **Ulysses**; *increase to dim lighting*

Cue 34   **Spirits** break away and cower back   (Page 30)
             Light begins to glow at far end of acting area—follow **Tiresias**
             and **Attendants**

Cue 35	**Sailors** overpower **Ulysses**	(Page 32)
	Fade light on **Tiresias** *and* **Attendants**	
Cue 36	**Sailors** carry **Ulysses** to ship	(Page 32)
	Increase lighting	
Cue 37	Wind increases	(Page 33)
	Spot on **Siren**	
Cue 38	**Sailors** row harder	(Page 34)
	Fade light on **Siren**	
Cue 39	As **Sailor** slides overboard	(Page 35)
	Lights rise and fall	
Cue 40	**Sailor**: "... we're through."	(Page 36)
	Steady lights	
Cue 41	Survivors settle down to row steadily	(Page 36)
	Fade down to spot on **Ulysses**	
Cue 42	**Sailor 4**: "An ox!"	(Page 37)
	Increase to day lighting	
Cue 43	**Ulysses I**: "Then a sombre cloud appeared ..."	(Page 39)
	Fade lighting	
Cue 44	**Sailors** stop rowing	(Page 39)
	Spot on **Poseidon** *high up*	
Cue 45	**Ulysses II**: "... rigging with it."	(Page 40)
	Cut spot on **Poseidon**	
Cue 46	**Ulysses** is swept bodily around	(Page 40)
	Flashes of lightning from time to time	
Cue 47	As movement slowly subsides	(Page 40)
	Gradually increase lighting	
Cue 48	**Ulysses** remains alone and unconscious	(Page 41)
	Light on mirror-ball as it spins; then fade to black-out	

ACT II

To open: House lights up

Cue 49	**Zeus** enters, followed by his **Secretary**	(Page 42)
	House lights down; bring up general lighting	
Cue 50	**Athene** and **Zeus** exit	(Page 47)
	Pause, then fade down to spot on **Ulysses**	
Cue 51	**Ulysses**: "... for the rest of time."	(Page 48)
	Increase lighting; fade spot on **Ulysses**	
Cue 52	**Athene**: "... are assembling already."	(Page 49)
	Fade lighting slightly	
Cue 53	**Seagulls** all sweep out	(Page 51)
	Fade to black-out	

Cue 54 As door opens in dark   (Page 51)
     Spill of light, pause, then close off light

Cue 55 **Telemachus**: "Mother?"   (Page 51)
     Bring up lighting on **Penelope**

Cue 56 **Telemachus**: "... I cannot see you."   (Page 52)
     Bring up dim lighting on **Telemachus** *and* **Athene**

Cue 57 **Athene**: "... believe all he tells you."   (Page 52)
     Repeat cue 54

Cue 58 **Suitors** weave their way out into the dark   (Page 53)
     Fade light on **Penelope**

Cue 59 **Athene** enters from another part   (Page 54)
     Cross-fade to lighting on **Ulysses**

Cue 60 **Ulysses** and **Telemachus** embrace   (Page 54)
     Cross-fade to **Ulysses I** and **II**

Cue 61 As SCENE 4 opens   (Page 55)
     Snap up general bright lighting

Cue 62 **Ulysses** swings across action   (Page 62)
     Lights down to strobe; floodlights on

Cue 63 **All Ulysses**: "... that is *now!*"   (Page 62)
     Strobe ends, lights return to normal, floodlights fade

Cue 64 **Athene**: "Therefore, be still ..."   (Page 64)
     After count of 5, light on mirror-ball as it revolves

Cue 65 All remain absolutely still   (Page 64)
     Fade to black-out

EFFECTS PLOT

ACT I

Cue 1   When ready   (Page 1)
Deep groaning, bass, profound, metallic, then mist swirls—continue mist

Cue 2   **Poseidon**: ". . . a liar and a trickster."   (Page 1)
Drum beats, steadily ominously

Cue 3   **Poseidon**: ". . . for all eternity."   (Page 2)
Thunder; drum beat quickens; noises of city at war—shouting, cries, clashing of weapons, crashing of buildings

Cue 4   As searchlights sweep floor   (Page 2)
Drum speeds up

Cue 5   More **Soldiers** arrive and move up towards city   (Page 2)
Increase battle noises and drums, plus music

Cue 6   As **Soldiers** advance   (Page 2)
Increase battle noises; continue mist

Cue 7   As **Refugees** enter   (Page 2)
Thunder, more drums

Cue 8   **Poseidon**: ". . . curse you, curse you . . .!"   (Page 2)
Huge wind; fade music, drums, battle noises

Cue 9   As **Sailors** start to row strongly   (Page 9)
Drums—long, steady beat, perhaps accompanied by music with strong, lyrical theme

Cue 10   As **Sailors** stop rowing   (Page 10)
Fade music and drums

Cue 11   As **Sailors** cry in alarm and lurch   (Page 11)
Noise as ship grounds

Cue 12   As rest of cast attack   (Page 11)
Drums crash and roll

Cue 13   Attackers exit   (Page 11)
Fade drums

Cue 14   **Sailor 9**: ". . . old Poseidon and his curses."   (Page 12)
Roll of thunder

Cue 15   As Lights fade up slowly to dawn   (Page 12)
Sound of rising wind

Cue 16   As **Sailors** embark and row again   (Page 12)
Music returns

Cue 17   **Poseidon**: "Take this!"   (Page 12)
           Increase wind

Cue 18   **Poseidon**: "And that!"   (Page 12)
           Increase wind still more

Cue 19   **Sailor 4**: "... the stars beneath us."   (Page 12)
           Fade wind and music

Cue 20   **Sailors** settle down for sleep   (Page 13)
           Soft North African music plays in distance

Cue 21   **Ulysses**: "... the land of the Lotus-Eaters."   (Page 13)
           Soporific music

Cue 22   **Crew**: "O—eeoh O!"   (Page 15)
           Wind comes up again, plus rowing music

Cue 23   As **Ulysses** and **Bosun** consult map   (Page 15)
           Fade wind and rowing music

Cue 24   **Sailors** wait   (Page 15)
           Slight sigh as boat lands

Cue 25   **Sailors** find places to settle; all is still   (Page 16)
           Single drumbeat

Cue 26   **Ulysses**: "... just staying at home."   (Page 16)
           Drumbeat

Cue 27   **Ulysses**: "... I heard it earlier."   (Page 16)
           *Drumbeat; pause for count of 5, then another drumbeat; more
           drumbeats ("footsteps") louder and quicker—fade as* **Sheep** *enter*

Cue 28   As **Ulysses** and **Bosun** plunge stake into **Cyclops'** eye   (Page 20)
           Sizzling sound; then drums, music

Cue 29   As **Ulysses** turns to audience   (Page 20)
           Fade drums and music

Cue 30   **Cyclops**: "... THAT ACCURSED GREEK!"   (Page 21)
           Drumbeats and thunder

Cue 31   **Sailor 3**: "... picking up a HUGE boulder——"   (Page 21)
           Faster drumbeats

Cue 32   **Sailor 4**: "... into the sea!"   (Page 21)
           Crash, thunder

Cue 33   As waves lie down to rest   (Page 22)
           Soft music—fade as Scene 5 begins

Cue 34   **Helmsman**: "... soon on our way."   (Page 23)
           Slight wind

Cue 35   **Sailors** open bag   (Page 23)
           Giant whoosh of wind; huge gale

Cue 36   **Sailor 10**: "Goodbye, dear native land."   (Page 23)
           Fade wind

Cue 37   **Circe** makes a gesture   (Page 27)
           Music plays

Cue 38   As Lights go down on feast   (Page 28)
             Fade music

Cue 39   **Ulysses**: "... special to everyone."   (Page 29)
             Ghostly music; sound of water dripping

Cue 40   **Sailors** retreat apprehensively   (Page 30)
             Slight wind moans and echoes

Cue 41   **Ulysses**: "Tiresias, come!"   (Page 30)
             Slow and inexorable drum beats—fade when **Tiresias** *and*
             Attendants *are in position*

Cue 42   As SCENE 8 begins   (Page 32)
             Slight wind; soft, seductive music comes and goes

Cue 43   They sail on contented for a while   (Page 33)
             Music returns, more loudly from another direction

Cue 44   **Ulysses**: "Did Tiresias not say——?"   (Page 33)
             Cut music

Cue 45   **Sailor 9**: "No, it's stopped."   (Page 33)
             Music, louder

Cue 46   **Ulysses**: "... as impulsive as ever!"   (Page 33)
             Wind increases

Cue 47   **Sailors** row   (Page 34)
             Another kind of music vies with the first

Cue 48   **Sailors** row harder; Light fades on **Siren**   (Page 34)
             After a while, fade music

Cue 49   **Ulysses**: "What challenge is this?"   (Page 34)
             Sound of racing water; wind rises

Cue 50   **Helmsman**: "Easier said than done!"   (Page 35)
             Deafening wind and sea

Cue 51   As **Sailor** slides overboard   (Page 35)
             Continue howling wind and sea, plus music and drums

Cue 52   **Sailor**: "... we're through!"   (Page 36)
             Wind dies down, also music and drums fade

Cue 53   **Sailor 5**: "Three oxen!"   (Page 37)
             Ox bellows off, followed by another and another

Cue 54   **Sun Cattle** enter   (Page 37)
             Soft music

Cue 55   As **Sailors** race down on herd   (Page 38)
             Fade music

Cue 56   **All**: "... we didn't know."   (Page 39)
             Growl of thunder in distance

Cue 57   **Sailors** start to row   (Page 39)
             Rowing music

Cue 58   **Sailors** stop rowing   (Page 39)
             Music breaks off

Cue 59	**Poseidon** releases sling-shot *Shrill whine*	(Page 40)
Cue 60	**Ulysses** is swept bodily around *Wind; storm sounds, music*	(Page 40)
Cue 61	As movement slowly subsides *Fade wind and storm noises; bring up soft, beguiling music*	(Page 40)

ACT II

Cue 62	Shortly after **Poseidon** enters *Gong, off*	(Page 42)
Cue 63	**Athene**: "... are assembling already." *Sea birds squawk, distantly*	(Page 49)
Cue 64	**Calypso**: "... our love will sustain you." *Increase sea birds sounds—continue*	(Page 49)
Cue 65	**Seagulls** all rise *Increase sea bird noise to very loud shrill shrieking; fade as* **Seagulls** *exit*	(Page 51)
Cue 66	As SCENE 3 begins *Fast music sweeps in; door opens, louder music, pause, door slams; decrease music*	(Page 51)
Cue 67	**Athene**: "... believe all he tells you." *Door opens, music increases, door closes, music decreases*	(Page 52)
Cue 68	**Telemachus** kneels and kisses hand *Fade music*	(Page 53)
Cue 69	**Athene**: "... keep your wits about you." *Great shrieking and calling of sea birds*	(Page 53)
Cue 70	**Seagulls**: "... failed, failed, failed ..." *Mournful cry of seagulls, fading out*	(Page 54)
Cue 71	As SCENE 4 begins *Fast music*	(Page 55)
Cue 72	**Others**: "The boar-hunt!" *Fade music*	(Page 55)
Cue 73	Court hold aloft metal rings (or curled fingers) *Drumbeats*	(Page 58)
Cue 75	**Antinuous**: "... the lady's heart at one!" *Drum beats faster*	(Page 60)
Cue 76	**All**: "What is Telemachus planning?" *Drum ends on a crash*	(Page 60)
Cue 77	**Ulysses** nods and walks slowly to his place *Steady thumping, off*	(Page 60)
Cue 78	Shortly after **Ulysses** fires arrow *Clang, off, followed by barking, off*	(Page 61)

Cue 79   **Ulysses**: "... to reclaim my own!"   (Page 61)
          Drumbeats and music to accompany action

Cue 80   **Ulysses** swings across on rope   (Page 62)
          Thunder cracks, drum crashes

Cue 81   Lights go to strobe   (Page 62)
          Trumpets and great shouting and fighting, off: more music,
          more thunder

Cue 82   **All Ulysses**: "... and that is *now*!"   (Page 62)
          Fade drumbeats, music and distant fighting

Cue 83   **Poseidon** (*on amplifier*): "Well ... all right."   (Page 63)
          Music—triumphant

Cue 84   **Zeus** reacts with horror   (Page 64)
          Fade music

PRODUCTION NOTES

With all this talk of *movement* in the script, what did I have in mind? The best thing is to try and look at rehearsals with the two casts that initiated the production.

*

Did you know that once upon a time young people didn't like to move? It's amazing but true. At youth club dances in the old days boys would line up on one side of the hall, girls on the other and both view with extreme suspicion and envy any who dared to cross the no-man's land in between. Nowadays, of course, if you watch any rock concert or disco, they seem to be moving non-stop. Indeed the difficulty is sometimes to make them stop.

And that is part of our problem.

For how do you channel all that frenetic energy into something creative and positive? *The Magical Voyage* was partly written to investigate that for the idea was to provide all kinds of opportunities for all kinds of movement, from mass stampedes to intimate mimes and dances. Today most drama societies have some kind of movement training, but my two casts were new to it all and had to start right at the beginning, learning, you might say, the very nuts and bolts of movement. So here are some of the things we had to do.

Warm-Ups. Even athletes must warm up. Nobody can go into free, enthusiastic movement without preparation. So rehearsals always started with warm-ups. Cast assembled in shorts, swimming trunks, singlets, leotards, whatever, loose, nothing restraining, bare feet if possible, standing with legs planted well apart (because that always gives authority and balance) starting to loosen up, first parts of the body in isolation, each sequence followed by small mimes to use that part in a meaningful activity. So starting with fingers and wrists, flicking, stretching, closing the fists, and then extending all the fingers, rotating the wrists first one way and then the other; and then with the other hand; and then both hands together, followed by simple mimes—sorting out a box of very sharp pins (be deft, don't prick yourself), take a watch to pieces, trail hands in water, put on a pair of very tight gloves, show old age hands, witch's hands and so on —all to encourage sensitivity just with hands and fingers. Remember that's all you're acting with at the moment, just hands and fingers. Then extend the movement up through the elbows into the upper arms and shoulders, stretching, writhing, windmilling, push a heavy object, climb an imaginary rope or cliff hauling yourself up with arms alone. Then on to one leg and loosen up the other leg in much the same way, stretching and flexing the toes (therefore bare feet are best), rotating the ankles, extend the action to the knee by flexing the hinge-joint of the knee, then to the thigh, bringing it right up to the chest to stretch the hamstrings. Then change feet and do the other leg. Follow with a few mimes for both legs and feet—walk on very thin ice, on a tightrope, on a very hot beach, walk into water deeper and deeper and feel how the action changes as the water climbs higher and higher. Or find the feet glued to the floor and struggle to move them—but don't worry too much about the rest of the body at present—now you are simply acting with the soles of your feet and legs.

Now the neck and head, nodding the head back and forth (gently, muscles and tendons are easily strained here) and then turning the head from side to side, all to exercise the two vertebrae at the top of the spinal column, the *atlas* and the *axis*, responsible for these movements, then rotating the head first one way and then the other, again gently, having respect for your body. Then the mimes—balancing imaginary books on your head, add to them and walk and sit; put on a dunce's hat, then swap it for a heavy crown. Now you are acting just with the top of your head. Struggle to free yourself from some medieval iron mask that presses and presses ... stretch the neck to look over a wall.

Now to the torso to link all these parts—stand with feet well apart and try and touch the walls without moving your feet, front, back, side and side and then rotating. Bend over as if to touch your toes, but keep your knees braced and don't force anything, let gravity pull your upper body down bit by bit. Now shower on a very hot day. Enjoy the experience, slow and languid. Now jump into a cold shower on a bitterly cold day—then towel off with alacrity, all over, quick, quick, quick. Consciously use the spine as you bend this way and that, really working with energy. Now use the spine as you wield a heavy axe over a log of wood, or dig up the garden with a pickaxe.

Finally link all the parts together using hands, strong feet and legs, neck and spine. Crouch down alongside a heavy bag of coal. With great effort hoist it on to your shoulders and stand with trembling legs. Walk with it, taking care its weight does not pull you backwards or push you over forwards. Now push a car up a hill—really work the body—or go for a walk through a haunted wood, pushing your way past spiderwebs, brambles and low hanging branches. Listen to music in your head and then conduct a huge orchestra with equally huge gestures. Be a goal-keeper, leaping and diving in all directions, and play Wimbledon tennis without a racquet.

After all this you can relax on to the floor. As you switch off muscle after muscle imagine a candle melting. Let yourself dissolve on to the floor—no, into the floor, using no hands to go down and making no sound. Then lie on your back and switch off everything—but *do not go to sleep.*

Exercises. Now we can put some of this to good use. Employing a few of the gestures we may have discovered in the limbering, we can explore the three levels of movement.* Most people are prepared to gesture at waist or shoulder height. It's comfortable and requires no great effort. But there are

---

* Much of this schedule has been developed from Rudolf Laban's theories of movement, which acknowledgement is gratefully made.

other levels—down at ankle height and high up, above the head. Discover these levels by clapping in them, then explore them with exercises e.g. unpack books from a crate on the floor and pack them as quickly as possible on shelves that extend right up above your head. Do this as rapidly as possible, constantly going from one extreme to the other. Then paint a wall with a large brush, jumping to reach the top of it and crouching down to paint the skirting board at floor level. Make all your gestures as large and sweeping as possible. All these levels are important and we should learn to move through them all with equal pleasure.

Hard and soft gestures might come next. Different gestures have different textures. Find a hard gesture for "Come here!" and follow it with a soft gesture for "*Please* come here." Similarly give hard and soft gestures for "Go away!" and "Please go away". Thrust with a sword. Compare that with, say, a comforting gesture. Try stabbing and dabbing, punching and petting. Then try starting with a hard gesture, but change it to a soft one half-way through. And reverse the process. Now try varying them on the different levels. And don't forget not only the hands can make gestures. Legs, feet, head, even the torso can make equally effective gestures. What else is stamping or nodding with the head? And if you've spent time limbering these parts, why waste them now?

And all of this might lead to open and closed gestures. Typical open gestures might indicate safety, happiness, victory, full tummies, anything secure. Closed gestures are usually identified with hunger, defeat, despair, illness, old age, anything insecure. Let the gestures come from the stomach, so that the open gestures really do open up the body. Then the closed gestures are a withering ... either fast or slow, or hard or soft depending on the motive you've given them. Then find open and closed positions for all parts of the body—hands, legs, necks and heads—and once again on all three levels. And don't forget to use the spines. Stretch them and make them work. They are the all-important linkage that make all these movements possible.

All this and more to get rid of anything that might inhibit a spontaneous movement. A young performer stands on a stage and says to himself (herself) "This feels awful. I can't move. My hands feel as big as cauliflowers, my feet are stuck to the floor. If only I could *move!*" All these exercises to get shot of that feeling, to let them move without embarrassment, turning self-consciousness (bad) into self-awareness (good). So we make them move. After a while we found they were too puffed to care, falling about with laughter, flushed and really raring to work. Or so it seems. With 180 degree spins and then 360 ones, leaps into the air, and being chased from one end of the hall to the other so they could become waves or seagulls or pigs and sailors and *enjoy* being them. And for all of them, constant work on the spine to learn how to row standing up or to draw an imaginary bow simply by transferring the weight from one part of the body to another....

So that's how it goes. The preparation. And not doing it only once but before every rehearsal. Every one. And if possible, before every performance as well.

But of course there are other things. It's not all movement.

Speech is certainly one of those other things. It's really amazing, I found, how many performers try to speak with their lips closed, mumble, mumble, mumble. It's as if the mere act of using the mouth is indecent. Yet everybody knows that to talk clearly you've got to use the mouth as a singer does, opening it to its fullest with tongue and lips working overtime to enunciate and project. So ... So we experimented with lip massage as well! Now that really does sound weird, rubbing the lips and limbering the muscles round the mouth by twisting the face into grotesque shapes, stretching and elongating it, and by working the tongue, flexing and extending and curling it, so that it becomes prepared to move. Like the larger muscles in the body, it grows lazy if not made to work, so that the epithet "lazy speech" is literally true. Then they challenged one another with the well-known tongue-twisters like "Betty Botter bought some butter, but the butter that she bought was bitter, so she bought some better butter, to make the bitter butter better". And then just working on selected vowels and consonants ... d, d, d, d ... t, t, t, t ... b, b, b, b, so that in the end the words would come ripping out with the force and pungency of machine-gun bullets.

Eyes can be exercised too and mental reactions sharpened with word games so that cues can be picked up smartly and returned like a tennis match played at high speed, quick, quick, quick!

What next?

Improvisations were certainly important for in spite of all this emphasis on gesture and movement, nothing was choreographed. Nothing looks worse than an imposed gesture. They've got to do it their way. They must find their own open and closed gestures, their own "textures". All we can do is make them aware of the possibilities. "You don't have to keep working on the same level, you know. You can stand on tiptoe, reach up above your head. And then swoop very, very low." That sort of thing. That's all these notes are for. After all they are the ones who have got to get up there and do it in front of an audience, so let them do it their way.

But there were other uses for the improvisations—working out the mechanics of some of the scenes. How to make the pigs different from the sheep, and the Magic Cattle different from the other two. How to make the seagulls "hover". As for those two monumental groups suggested in the opening scene, symbolizing the victory of the Greeks and the defeat of Troy, here is ideal work for open and closed gestures on a group scale, but the cast seemed to know instinctively how to put them together. I just got in the way there.

Finally to the obvious things—*set, costumes, make-up*. Very little was used in the way of scenery. Indeed as much clear space as possible was left for the large running moves, perhaps one end of the acting area could be marked with potted plants and used for the Circe and Calypso scenes, another marked with rocks and so on for the Cyclops and Hades scenes with a rostrum or ramp linking the two for the ship. One of the productions was certainly Greek, because I had recently done productions of *The Trojan Horse* and *Alexander the Great* and knew where I could lay my hands on some Greek bits and pieces including some plumed helmets and short-bladed swords. Apart from that, the casts came up with their own ideas.